C000243227

KENT
MURDER
CASEBOOK

W. H. JOHNSON

COUNTRYSIDE BOOKS
NEWBURY · BERKSHIRE

COUNTRYSIDE BOOKS
3 Catherine Road
Newbury, Berkshire

ISBN 1 85306 522 6

Map by Trevor Yorke

Produced through MRM Associates Ltd., Reading
Typeset by Techniset Typesetters, Newton-le-Willows
Printed by Woolnough Bookbinding Ltd., Irthlingborough

CONTENTS

ACKNOWLEDGEMENTS

I am grateful to many people who have been of help to me in the preparation of this book. In particular, I should like to mention members of Kent Arts and Libraries who have been unfailingly efficient, especially Penny Ward of Margate Library and David Cousins of Canterbury Library. Sincere thanks are also owed to Simon Finch of Bromley Central Library; Lorna Kenward of Eastbourne Reference Library; Piers Morgan, Photographic Editor, *Medway News*; Roger Perkins, Editor, and Alex Watson, photographer, *Sevenoaks Chronicle*; Cathy Tyce, *Kent Messenger* Group; Marie Elmer of Clifford Elmer Books, Cheadle; and Superintendent John Hann of Kent County Constabulary.

I should like also to place on record my reliance on the work of many journalists, past and present, and to thank them for making the writing of this book so interesting. I hope that I have adequately acknowledged their contributions in the text.

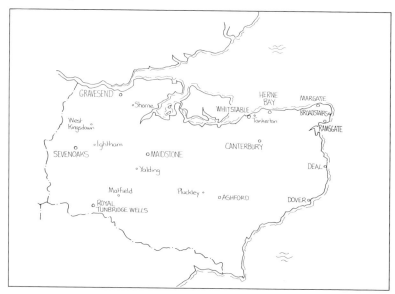

INTRODUCTION

All the crimes described in this book took place in the county of Kent. But they could have been committed in any place and at any time. There is nothing especially Kentish about these or any other crimes for that matter. Each of them, however, has the drama, the narrative drive, that seems to invest even the most banal of murder cases.

The cases were selected in the hope that they would present a range of killings and perhaps to raise questions about degrees of wickedness for, despite the appalling nature of most of the deeds, some of those who killed are patently worse than others.

Perhaps killing, rather than murder, is a better word to employ because at least two of the deaths were the result, according to the judge and jury, of men reacting violently but not being guilty of murder. In one instance, under the mistaken belief that he was being attacked on his own property, the accused stabbed his victim to death. In another case, the estranged husband's gun went off as he struggled with his wife's lover. And of course while all of the other cases can safely be described as murders not all of them were satisfactorily concluded, for either the killer was never found or suicide prevented the suspect being brought before the courts. In one case described here the prime suspect has evaded police questioning by remaining outside British jurisdiction.

And then there are the cases of those who are not responsible for their actions and in one of these it is legitimate to ask if, had the authorities been more alert, might the dreadful frenzies of a serial killer have been avoided? Yet perhaps it is a cheap solution, too easily come by, to batten responsibility onto the major agencies. So frequently even the most dangerous in our midst are not obviously on the point of creating mayhem.

Some of the murders described in this book were committed out of some warped and absurd desire for revenge or in the hope of modest financial rewards. There are several such cases, three of them committed by immature adolescents. These are the everyday kinds of crime, the motives of which whilst deplorable are easy for us to

5

understand. But what is inexplicable and remains a constant puzzle is the totally unexpected murder in Ashford Hospital which seems, as far as the guilty man is concerned, so out of character. What was it that sparked off, apparently out of the blue, his desire to kill a seeming stranger inside the hospital buildings? That such an ordinary man, happily married, the father of two very young children, should come to murder is unsettling.

But in the end it is the four high profile murders which have about them the most chilling quality. Sidney Fox murdered his mother for gain. George Joseph Smith disposed of three women – or at least we know of three – for gain. And if Harriet Staunton and her baby were not murdered, how else can the deaths of this frail creature and the year-old Tommy be described? Certainly they underwent privations of starvation and neglect that go deep beyond the boundaries of simple cruelty. Again financial gain seems to be at the root of the vile treatment to which the mother was systematically treated. But why the child? What is it that marks off these killers for gain from the boy in the Plaza Cinema who murdered the manager for a few pounds? It is not the sums of money involved: that seems evident. They are all after cash. But we are not talking about some bumbling adolescent murder when dealing with Fox or Smith or the killers of Staunton. Their offences are of a grosser quality. For each of them murders a victim who trusts them. These murderers have about them an emptiness of soul, a deadness of feeling. They are the worst of all, these cold killers. Sidney Fox comes back from a visit to London with a gift, a bottle of port, for his doting mother. As far as Smith's deluded brides were concerned, they were on their honeymoon, poor, sad, trusting souls.

But in the Staunton case perhaps the depths are reached. Right to the last not the slightest kindness was offered to the weak-minded wife who only a day or so before she died had lost the baby she loved, a victim of the same calculated wickedness that she had suffered for months. The thought lingers that Harriet Staunton might to the very end have deluded herself that her husband loved her. At least Fox's mother, having drunk half of the bottle of port he had brought her, is thought not to have known much about her last minutes. And apparently Smith's method of despatching his brides was quickly effective. But Harriet Staunton's death was slow and in that tiny house where she spent her last months, her husband, her brother-in-law and his wife and her husband's mistress could not fail to know what they were doing so deliberately. These people freeze the blood.

And the fourth high profile case I have chosen is the murder, by person or persons unknown, of seven year old Georgina Moore. There was a much publicised trial and the accused, Esther Pay, was finally acquitted. Surely it could not have been Esther who led the seven year old along those dark and lonely country lanes to the very banks of the Medway. She loved Georgina and in turn the child loved her. Could Esther Pay have betrayed her in such a way? It is inconceivable. And yet, Esther had been, perhaps at the time of the murder she still was, the lover of Georgina's father. And the circumstantial evidence weighs heavily against her. If she was guilty of this crime then Esther Pay must join the other bleakly cruel and treacherous murderers who have deliberately taken a route that marks them out as among the worst of their kind.

And finally, what is it that leads us to want to know about these people, especially the worst of them? The cases at Stella Maris, at Matfield and at the Chinese Lantern Café are banal enough in their way. In a sense they are the stuff of a thousand soaps but what makes such a dismissive phrase inappropriate is that here were real folk of flesh and blood, some of them suffering deeply from the jealousy of dead or dying relationships. We all know of disastrous failing marriages or love affairs. Mercifully, they do not all lead to murder though the intensity of the passions may well be as deep as those suffered by the principals in each of these cases.

So perhaps it is the recognition of the states of mind, the attitudes, the situations, the motives or responses of those involved in killing another human being that provokes our interest. Is it to ask questions of ourselves, to consider our own darkest thoughts, that we are interested in these crimes? Or is it a desire to look sometimes far over the edge and into an abyss, in whose grim depths we can perhaps discern those whose disturbing actions are for all time beyond our sympathy and understanding but which nevertheless intrigue us?

W. H. Johnson

1

THE
FORTUNE HUNTERS

The murder of Harriet Staunton at Cudham,
April 1877

Poor Harriet Butterfield did not have a suitor until she was in her thirties. So why, when one finally did come along, did her mother try to stop her marrying him? It seemed so unfair to Harriet – so unfair, in fact, that she went to live with an aunt. Her mother then tried to have her committed as a lunatic and failed; tried to have her made a ward in Chancery and failed.

What motivated Mrs Butterfield? Did she fear that young Lewis Staunton was after her daughter's fortune? The first Married Women's Property Act had been passed only shortly before to prevent that sort of thing. Did she think Lewis had found a loophole?

In spite of her mother, in June 1875 Harriet married Lewis, an auctioneer's clerk of 24, ten years her junior.

Mrs Butterfield went on worrying. She knew her daughter was of very weak intellect, quite incapable of managing her own affairs. Swallowing her pride she paid the young couple a visit at their home at 8 Loughborough Road, Brixton, three weeks after the wedding. She stayed only a quarter of an hour but they parted, as she thought, on reasonable terms.

The following day, however, Mrs Butterfield received a letter from Lewis forbidding her the house and any further contact with her daughter. A note from Harriet supported her husband. Mrs Butterfield was never to see Harriet again.

Later in the year when Harriet became pregnant, 20 year old Alice Rhodes came to live at Loughborough Road. Alice's sister, Lizzie, was married to Lewis's brother, Patrick. Ostensibly she had come to help

Harriet Staunton shortly after her marriage in 1875.

Harriet during her pregnancy. In truth, she had been Lewis's mistress before his marriage and was to remain so. Clara Brown, a 16 year old who acted as a servant to her two cousins, Alice and Lizzie, was also at Loughborough Road for some of the time. She said later that Lewis and Alice showed each other 'a great deal more affection than was necessary'.

Mrs Butterfield's suspicions about her son-in-law's motives for marrying Harriet had certainly been correct. In March 1876 the couple's son, Thomas Henry Staunton, was born. More important to Lewis, however, was the fact that £1,177 15s 2d was transferred into his bank account from Harriet's Trust Fund. In the next month £639 4s 1d took the same route, followed in July by £310 4s 6d. And there was more to come.

Perhaps it was because Harriet could not adequately care for the child that Tommy was sent to live with Lewis's younger brother, Patrick, a professional artist, and his wife Lizzie. They had recently moved from Brixton to the remote and beautiful village of Cudham, near Bromley. Here their two-up, two-down cottage, Woodlands, lay well back from the road, the rear and sides of the dwelling being heavily wooded. The nearest of their very few neighbours was 300 yards away. Clara Brown was there much of the time and Lewis often stayed there, sometimes with Alice, occasionally with Harriet.

Lewis was busy. Using his wife's money he had established himself as an auctioneer in Gipsy Hill, where he and Harriet now moved. But what ought to have been for the young man an exciting time, with a new baby and a new business, he found less than congenial. A letter written in late June 1876 to Patrick – he calls him 'Bay' – gives an indication of this.

'No one knows, my dear Bay, what I have had to put up with from Harriet the last six months. Her temper has been something frightful. I have talked to her for hours together and tried to reason with her but it is all of no use. From the time she gets up in the morning until she goes to bed at night, she does nothing but aggravate and make me as miserable as she possibly can … I have been quite disheartened and cried for hours to think I should have laid out money to make things nice and have no one to take any interest in the place. I am, indeed, truly unhappy.'

Even if Harriet had on occasion a bad temper – and there is some evidence of this – Lewis should have remembered that most of his money came from her; that competent mother or no, her child had gone from her; and that it was apparent even to her that something was going on between Alice and Lewis.

Some time in August Harriet went to stay at Woodlands. But perhaps Patrick and Lizzie, too, found her a trial at times. A letter from Lewis dated 28th August refers to Patrick's 'two dear children' who are ill. 'I want you to send Harriet up tomorrow for I am sure you cannot be bothered with her just now,' he writes, 'and I will then send Alice down to help dear Lizzie.' Certainly, Lewis seems to have had some affection for his brother's wife and children.

Three days later, Harriet was still at Cudham – in fact, she was never to leave – and Lewis was apologising to Patrick again. 'I feel so sorry Harriet should have given you so much trouble. What to do with her, I do not know.'

At this time, Lewis was paying his brother £1 a week for Harriet's keep. She stayed on, tolerated, lonely, seeing her husband some weekends. A letter from her in September suggests her loneliness and her hope of returning home to Gipsy Hill. The letter hints, too, at some domestic casualness.

'My own darling,

I write these few lines hoping they will find you well. Will you be down on Sunday? If not I shall be disappointed. Hope to see you on Monday. If not let me know which day you will be down. Will you bring me down please peace [sic] ribon [sic] and frilling for my colour [collar] and selves [sleeves]. I hope to return to town with you soon. Tommy is quite well, so goodnight, my dear, God bless you. I have not had a clean flannel for a month on Saturday. It is time I shall be at home. My boots has worn out.

From your ever affectionate wife,

Harriet.'

Harriet continued to dream of the day when she and Tommy would return to Gipsy Hill, unaware that in October Lewis had sold the Gipsy Hill business and moved to Little Greys Farm, only a mile from Woodlands. Alice, now pregnant, moved in with him, passing herself off as his wife.

Patrick and Lizzie played their part in this deception. Had they conspired, all of them, and determined the way out for Lewis? After all,

Woodlands where Harriet Staunton and her baby were starved to death.

11

he now had most of his wife's property - there was just one more transaction to make, after which time she would be no more to them than an obstacle and a nuisance.

A bequest to Harriet of £2,000 was to be made over to Lewis and it was necessary that this be done legally before a Commissioner in London. As a married woman she could only dispose of her property if the Commissioner was satisfied that she was doing so of her own free will.

For Harriet, then, there were a couple of outings to London with Lewis. On their visit on 17th October she was in such a nervous state that the negotiation could not be completed. All was satisfactory on the visit of 23rd October, however, when she signed away the last of her fortune, although the Commissioner was later to admit that he had been slightly worried about bruises around Harriet's eyes.

Then came a new phase in the life of Harriet Staunton. From now on she was rarely seen. Between October 1876 and April 1877 only two people outside the family, a gamekeeper and a visiting fishmonger, caught sight of her. At Christmas time two girls who called at the house heard her footsteps in the kitchen. None of these people, however, had any knowledge of who she was.

Over Christmas, Harriet and Tommy were left in the care of young Clara Brown. Patrick and Lizzie were away for several days; Lewis did not come to see his wife and child. She made no effort to leave Woodlands, presumably by now accepting that she was to stay there.

After Christmas, Harriet no longer joined the others downstairs. She was confined to a bedroom, 13 feet 2 inches by 8 feet 2 inches, that she shared with Clara, Tommy and one of Patrick's babies. Clara Brown was to relate in court how Patrick, a vicious young man, once called out to her, 'You must not come downstairs, you - - - cat, or I will break your neck.'

In February 1877 Mrs Butterfield, who had written without success to Lewis, managed to meet Alice Rhodes at London Bridge station. Alice was not especially helpful; after all, her lover hated Harriet's mother. She first told Mrs Butterfield she did not know where Harriet was and later told her she was with Lewis in Brighton. Her daughter was happy, Mrs Butterfield was told. 'You should see her playing with little Tommy; it is great fun.'

But it was not great fun. By then Harriet was increasingly incapable of playing with Tommy. And Tommy was increasingly incapable of being played with.

Mrs Butterfield persevered, still hoping to see her daughter. She met Patrick, too, at London Bridge station but he threatened her. 'If you come to my house,' he told her, 'I'll blow your brains out.'

Undeterred, the old woman made her way to Cudham, arriving at Little Greys Farm where she believed Harriet to be. Lewis refused her entry. 'If you would only let me hear her voice or see her hand on the balustrade,' she pleaded, 'I should know that she was in her proper place.'

'You will never see her if you live for a thousand years,' her son-in-law told her.

Mrs Butterfield next asked the local police to watch Little Greys Farm and report any sign of Harriet to her. They did keep a watch for some weeks but naturally, as Harriet was at Woodlands, they were unable to offer her mother any comforting news.

Matters came to a head shortly afterwards. On 10th April, Patrick and Lizzie took Tommy into Guy's Hospital. Lewis stayed outside. They told the nurse that the child was ill, the mother being incapable of looking after him. Little Tommy, a year old now, was wearing the clothes of a month old child. Patrick returned to the hospital the next day with appropriate clothing, to learn that Tommy had died of starvation.

Lewis, now using the name John Harris and claiming to be acting on behalf of the child's family, arranged the funeral. He did not want it to be expensive, he said. The child's name was entered in the register as Henry Stornton.

The following day, 12th April, it was decided that something had to be done about Harriet who was by now too ill to comprehend that her baby was dead. A druggist at Westerham refused to prescribe medicine, advising them to see a doctor. Instead Lewis, Patrick and Lizzie immediately left Harriet in the care of Alice. They went by train from Bromley to Penge where they rented two rooms in Forbes Road. Here they told the landlady, Mrs Chalkin, that later in the day they would be bringing an invalid lady to stay. She was not desperately ill they said.

On Mrs Chalkin's recommendation the trio went to Dr Longrigg, a local practitioner. They wished him to visit a lady who would be arriving later in the day. They described her as 'extremely thin but healthy' and 'cleanly in her habits.'

They returned to Cudham and by seven o'clock in the evening were bundling the dying Harriet, violently shaking, incapable of walking and constantly groaning, into a wagonette. Alice Rhodes joined the other three on the six mile journey to Bromley station where they took the train to Penge. About nine o'clock the party reached Mrs Chalkin's. The landlady was horrified at what she saw. They had said the lady was not desperately ill but she was obviously so.

Lewis now decided to postpone the doctor's visit. 'The case is not as bad as all that,' he said. 'We will wait till the morning.'

Calm enough, one has to say, for a man whose wife was on the point of death and whose baby boy had died the previous day.

Harriet Staunton died the next morning and Dr Longrigg signed a certificate giving the cause of death as apoplexy. Lewis, anxious to wind matters up, made the funeral arrangements. The funeral was to be properly carried out, he said, but not too expensive. Leaving the corpse with Mrs Chalkin and attempting to reassure her that Harriet had been a neighbour who until recently had been in good health, the party returned to Cudham.

When Harriet's family heard of her death her brother-in-law demanded a post mortem. The inquest produced facts too horrifying to ignore. The nurse stated: 'I went to wash the body but it was so dirty I could not. The head was alive with lice ... It was a sort of dirt on the body that appeared to have belonged to the bark of a tree and had been growing for a long time.'

Dr Longrigg withdrew his original certificate, and now stated that Harriet had died from starvation exacerbated by the journey to Penge. To this he added neglect and exhaustion. 'The body was fearfully emaciated and filthily dirty all over,' he said. 'It weighed 5 stone 4 lb ... There was comparatively no breast.'

Inevitably, Lewis and Patrick, Lizzie and Alice were charged with murder. In Newgate whilst awaiting their trial at the Old Bailey – where it was thought a 'more calm, dispassionate and unimpassioned judgment would be formed in their case' than in Kent – both women gave birth.

The trial report makes grim reading. It is a tale of casual indifference, gross callousness, frightening threats, occasional violence and calcu-lated cruelty. Clara Brown in particular attested to Patrick's hitting Harriet as well as Tommy and his own wife.

The defence was based on the cause of death. Medical experts were called to assert that it was possible that Harriet had died from tubercular meningitis. Whilst they did not condone the neglect, they would not accept Longrigg's assumption as to the cause of death.

Unsurprisingly the jury returned a verdict of guilty. The judge spoke of 'barbarity', of 'a poor, innocent, outraged woman', and told the four prisoners that although they had not been charged with Tommy's death, 'I cannot help feeling satisfied within my own mind that you are guilty of contemplating and plotting and having brought about his death.' All four were sentenced to hang at Maidstone.

Then the campaigns began. Seven hundred doctors signed a document declaring a lack of conviction in the post mortem conclusion. *The Lancet* insisted that before proving murder by starvation it was necessary to prove death by starvation, and that had not been done. At Maidstone, the Association for the Abolition of Capital Punishment held a meeting pleading for the lives of the four condemned. Letters, columns of them, appeared in all the national newspapers, many of them attacking the medical evidence.

The doubts cast upon the verdict influenced the Home Secretary, and the capital sentences were revoked. Alice Rhodes was released. Lewis, Patrick and Lizzie Staunton were to remain in prison for the rest of their natural lives.

Still the questions remain. It is to be assumed that Patrick and his wife Lizzie, bearing much of the burden, were going to share Lewis's new-found fortune. But whose idea was it in the first place? And when was it first conjured up? How could these relatively well-educated, respectable people do what they did? Did no one ever have any pity for Tommy? Or for Harriet? What sort of people were these?

2

A LONG WALK ON A
WINTER'S NIGHT

The murder of Georgina Moore at Yalding,
December 1881

They get off the train at Paddock Wood, the woman and the little girl, arriving there from Charing Cross at 4.10 pm. It is a grey, drizzling afternoon, only five days before the Christmas of 1881. Over at the nearby stables the woman asks Charles Barton, the fly-proprietor, the fare to Yalding. When he tells her it will be 4s, she is surprised. Yes, he tells her, it is four miles but there will be a train along shortly. It will take them to Yalding for only 3d. She does not want to go there by train, the woman says, and she walks off. The child runs along beside her. And if she goes to Yalding that way, Barton thinks, she's going the long way round.

A little further on, just by the Kent Arms, the ostler, Charles Cronk, fancies he recognises the woman in the ulster coat. He hears her call out, 'Come along, my dear' and watches the two figures walk on.

A mile beyond, Samuel James, standing outside the Elm Tree, sees a woman, about 36 years old, in a light ulster 'with a bit of black stuff round her hat'. There is a girl with her. They pass him. There is a fog now; the air is raw; the road, apart from themselves, is empty; the sky darkens.

Nearly another mile and at the Queen's Head, Brenchley, a heavily-veiled woman calling in for a glass of gin stands in the shadows just inside the door. Then it is onto the road again, a lovely road in daylight, but in this early evening all is obscured. There are no stars; there is no moon.

Some time that evening, the woman, the skirts of her dress now heavily stained with mud, takes the child into the New Inn at

Laddingford. Here, she buys three penn'orth of whisky against the winter evening's chill and the little girl, clearly very tired according to the landlord, has some cake. Shortly after seven o'clock, they leave.

During that winter's evening George Bradley, living at Yalding, a good couple of miles from the New Inn, thinks he hears a cry in the night but he dismisses it as a fox barking or a rabbit screaming its life away.

This is a beautiful stretch of country, this Upper Medway valley, and Yalding is a pretty village, with its oasts, its weatherboarded houses, its church with the off-centre dome.

And its river.

*   *   *

When Georgina did not arrive home from school, her mother began to worry. It was so unlike the child; she was so obedient. Eventually at eight o'clock Mrs Moore sent for her estranged husband who was working overtime as a carpenter at Drummond's Bank in nearby Spring Gardens. She explained to him how at 1.30 Georgina had gone off, holding a halfpenny in her hand to buy a cake. She hadn't come back.

Georgina Moore.

17

Despite searching the Pimlico streets for hours, calling on police, neighbours and friends, there was no sign of the seven year old, neither that night nor the following day. The only information came from a little boy. Yes, he had seen Georgina after dinner on the way to school. She was with a tall lady wearing a light ulster coat.

A light ulster? A tall lady? Esther Pay? Could it be her? It sounded like her. And Georgina loved Esther who had often taken her out and bought her sweets and toys. But the response from Esther Pay when she was called on by Mary Moore was cold. No, she had not seen Georgina.

Perhaps such coldness was understandable. There had been some difficulty between the Moores and the Pays. At one time they had lived in the same house, William Pay, a wheelwright, being the landlord. A couple of years earlier, however, when Pay had heard that his wife and Moore were lovers, he had turned his tenants out. Not that that ended the liaison. The Moores had gone to live not far away at 105 Winchester Street. When in July 1881 Pay discovered that he was still being cuckolded, he gave his wife a brutal beating. Moore now severed the relationship, according to him for Esther's sake. But Esther had not wished the affair to end. Was she now showing her resentment at how

Engravings of Stephen Moore and Esther Pay.

18

matters had turned out, when her former lover's wife appeared on the doorstep on 21st December?

If William Pay was a brutal drunk, Esther had hardly chosen a paragon in Stephen Moore. He was a relentless womaniser. Some years earlier he had been known as Harry Williams to Emma Irwin in Bath and father to her short-lived son; presumably he used the same name when he made her sister, Alice Dunn, pregnant. Now, however, he was living in Regents Park with Mrs Maidment and seeing a Miss Carrol, a servant girl, some nights. Most likely he was paying attention to others unknown at the same time.

Despite her initial frosty response, Esther's association with Stephen Moore began again in late December 1881, just after Georgina's disappearance. For the next few weeks they met regularly, lovers once more. As early as 23rd December, Moore asked Esther if she had any responsibility for his daughter's disappearance. No, she said, but she knew that tongues were wagging about her and Georgina. When Moore reminded her that she had once said that if they ended their affair she would steal Georgina and bring her up herself, she replied that she had been joking. In any event, she told him, she had been out with friends on the day in question. She had an alibi.

It was not until 5th January 1882 that Inspector Henry Marshall from Scotland Yard went to see Esther Pay.

'Why have you called on me?' she asked the policeman.

'Because the rumours are you have taken the child away,' he told her.

Turning to Moore who had accompanied the policeman, she said, 'You know where I was on the 20th. I was with Carrie Rutter.'

The next day Inspector Marshall returned to the house unaccompanied. When Esther came to the door, he heard a man's voice call out.

'Who is it?"

'That's my husband,' she told her visitor. 'He's in bed drunk and he thinks you are Moore and you had better leave.' Again Marshall had learnt little for his pains.

For the next few weeks the police made unavailing enquiries. They had no body, no witnesses. Georgina had simply gone, leaving no trace.

In the meantime, though seemingly worried about his child, Moore continued to live with Mrs Maidment, to console his wife and to meet Miss Carrol and Esther.

On 25th January, Esther left her husband and moved into lodgings in

Lower Sloane Street where she assumed the name Black. Possibly this was so that she could meet her lover more easily. Or was it that her husband, who was now publicly stating that his wife had some responsibility for Georgina's disappearance, had thrown her out? Alternatively, was it that she was hounded out of the district by those who believed she knew what had happened to the child?

This move was of short duration for she had decided to leave London and to go to her parents' house and then perhaps take a post as a servant in a gentleman's house. On Saturday 28th January, Moore met Esther at Charing Cross station. They had a glass of wine; he bought her some flowers and gave her a copy of *The Penny Illustrated* to read on the train. While she looked after her luggage, which included a birdcage, Moore went to get her ticket to Yalding. From there it would be a short journey to Nettlestead where her parents lived. On 28th January, the day of Esther's visit to her parents' house, *The Penny Illustrated* carried the following insert:

MISSING

From Pimlico, since noon, 20th ult., GEORGINA MOORE, age $7\frac{1}{2}$ years, tall for her age, complexion very fair, with bright colour, hair golden with fringe on forehead, eyes blue; dress, dark blue serge frock, dark ulster with two rows of black buttons, white straw hat trimmed with black velvet, dark blue knitted stockings; button boots.

A reward of £10 was offered by the Home Office, £5 by Stephen Moore and £25 by a London auctioneer, Mr Ingram.

It was too late. *The Times* of Tuesday 31st January carried the following:

SHOCKING DISCOVERY – At half past four yesterday afternoon the dead body of a little girl was taken out of the river Medway close to the South Eastern Railway Station at Yalding near Maidstone under circumstances which have led to the belief that the deceased was identified with a little girl named Georgina Moore ... The appearance of the body, which had evidently been in the water a considerable time, leads to strong suspicions of foul play. The neck is much marked, as if death had been produced by strangulation, and round the body was fixed some wire attached to a brick, evidently used to sink the corpse.

The cottage at Nettlestead, where Esther Pay was arrested, as it looks today.

On that Tuesday, Stephen Moore accompanied Inspector Marshall to Yalding, identifying Georgina's body in an outhouse of the New Inn.

Marshall then went to nearby Nettlestead where Esther had been staying with her mother and father since the previous Saturday. He detained her on suspicion of stealing the child. She might even, he said, be charged with murder.

'Well,' she replied, 'you must prove it.'

Doubtless Marshall was pondering a letter he had found while searching Esther's bedroom. She had intended to send it to Moore.

'Darling,' it read, 'I arrived home quite safely later than I expected. My brother met me at the station. Found all well except my mother. Dear, write me a few lines, I think so much of you in your trouble. I seem so far from you now. If you hear tidings let me know at once. Poor little darling. I hope you will find her ... Oh, darling, it is so dull here. I'm afraid I cannot stay long. I will see you if you want me ...'

There was, however, a marked change in Esther's attitude by the time she reached Yalding police station on the day of her arrest. When told that Georgina's body had been found in the water just below the footpath which led to her parents' house, she was ready to suggest that Moore knew more than he was saying. After all, no one knew her address at Nettlestead apart from the Moores and her husband.

21

'And it's very strange to me if Moore doesn't know something about it. He's so artful. You'd better look after him for I shouldn't be surprised if he's not missing very shortly. I know he's not on very good terms with his wife and now he's got rid of Georgina you'd better look very sharp after him, for if once he gets away, you'll never catch him.'

Would she, she asked, have brought a child and murdered her here? She had no doubt someone was trying to place the blame on her.

'Will he ride in the carriage with us?' Esther asked Marshall as they stood on the platform at Yalding to make the return to London. Learning that she and Moore were to be kept apart, she said, 'Well, don't be surprised if he bolts and then you'll find the most guilty party is gone.'

Later, suggesting perhaps that Moore's West Country lady friends, Emma Irwin and Alice Dunn, might be involved in some plot, she warned Marshall, 'You'd better stop any telegrams to Bristol.' She developed this theme on the train journey, that one of Moore's deceived lady friends had sought revenge on him through his daughter.

'He has served women very badly – some that I know worse than me – and he has served me bad enough,' she told the Inspector. 'Why don't you discover them and then you might get on the right track?'

When at last the lovers came face to face in Wimbledon police station, Moore had changed his mind about Esther's innocence. Till now he had ignored the rumours but no longer. Not since his daughter's body had been found at Yalding. 'I think you must be implicated,' he told her.

At a summary hearing at Westminster, the findings of the post mortem were revealed. The child had died of strangulation and not drowning. There was no water in her lungs. In the stomach there was some undigested starchy food – potato, bread or rice.

After hearing a number of witnesses, Esther was remanded to the Lewes Assizes where it was felt that she would receive a fairer trial than in outraged Kent.

Georgina Moore was buried at Brompton Cemetery on Saturday 4th February 1882. Over 2,000 people gathered in Winchester Street to see the hearse. There was obvious sympathy for Mary Moore but when her husband appeared the crowd 'groaned and hissed' and the police had some difficulty in restraining them. Moore was the villain of the piece, that much was clear; he was the author of his daughter's woes, no matter if he had not murdered her. Throughout the burial service, he was locked in the mortuary for his own safety.

The trial of Esther Pay took place at Lewes from 27th April to 1st May 1882. She appeared before Baron Pollock; was prosecuted by Messrs Poland, Biron and Eyre Lloyd and defended by Edward Clarke. Esther impressed the onlookers. She was 'a fine-looking, well-dressed woman, who appeared perfectly self-composed and, upon the charge being read to her, answered in a firm voice "Not guilty".'

It was the prosecution's case that Esther Pay had murdered Georgina to avenge herself upon Stephen Moore. It was a lengthy and complicated case, but in effect there were three major matters to be considered: identification, Esther's alibi and the possibility that another of Stephen's womenfolk was guilty.

Edward Clarke's cross-examination of Moore was to show that the man in the witness box encouraged women to hate him. Could not another aggrieved lover have spirited Georgina away?

The identification of the woman with the child who had walked from Paddock Wood station to Yalding was uncertain. The fly-proprietor could not say if it was Esther who had asked him the fare to Yalding. He was not even sure about the day or which side of Christmas it fell.

The 19 year old ostler at the Kent Arms who thought the woman familiar had not seen Esther for ten years. At the identity parade he had failed to recognise her. Samuel James who had seen a woman pass the Elm Tree did not pick out Esther at Lewes Gaol, nor did the wife of the landlord at the Queen's Head where the woman had bought a glass of gin. In fact, only one witness identified Esther as the woman in the Queen's Head.

Arthur Harrington, a seven year old, believed he had seen Esther with Georgina in Pimlico after dinner on 20th December, as did Police Constable Hill. Their testimony did not, however, place Esther or the child in Kent.

Two women were sure that they saw Esther with her mother on the platform at Yalding station on 21st December. Her parents, brother and sister-in-law, however, had all denied that she had been at Nettlestead on 20th December. The women were mistaken, the family members said. The meeting on the platform had taken place earlier in the year. After all, Mrs Humphreys, Esther's mother, had been too ill to go out in December. Her husband, a well respected hop orchard bailiff, was in no doubt about this.

Of course, unknown to her family Esther might well have been in Yalding on 20th December but returned to London on the train that left Yalding at 8.48 or 9.22 pm.

Mr Edward Clarke, whose speech in Esther Pay's defence was a masterpiece.

Nevertheless, two witnesses who called at the Pay house in Pimlico on the morning of 21st December found Esther not at home. There is no indication of where she was at that time and this flawed aspect of her alibi was not pursued adequately by the prosecution. It could have presented some problems for the defence.

Esther's claims to have spent the afternoon of 20th December at the Aquarium with Emma Harris and the night at the shops in Fulham and Hammersmith with Carrie Rutter were also denied by both women. No one had seen her in London that afternoon or evening.

Ignoring the weaknesses of her alibi, Edward Clarke's closing speech to the jury was a masterpiece. Would a woman commit such a barbarous crime? Could a woman commit such a crime? Surely only a man would have the nerve and physical skill to murder a child, bind her with wire and throw her into the river. And after all, Esther had no motive: Moore had only separated from her to save her from her violent husband. She had no reason to seek revenge and certainly not in such a monstrous manner. In any case, Esther had loved Georgina, and the child had loved her. It was Clarke's opinion that the child was murdered in Pimlico, the body bundled into a case and then conveyed to Yalding.

Clarke created doubt in the jurors' minds. They began to wonder if only a man could have done this murder. And if so, which man?

Whilst the judge's summing up was inclined to weigh the scales against Esther, the jury ignored his suggestions. After 20 minutes they returned a verdict of not guilty. Edward Clarke had offered a brilliant defence, but Esther Pay must have persuaded the jury of her innocence very powerfully. Or was it that Stephen Moore cut so unsymphathetic a figure? How else can the jury's hasty verdict be accounted for, considering the circumstantial evidence?

Who, then, did murder seven year old Georgina Moore, a 'nice little thing, dressed in the ordinary way for school by her mother who never after saw her alive'?

Had the body been thrown in the water at Yalding deliberately in order to implicate Esther? This is too fanciful. The wire and the brick attached to the body were intended to keep it on the bottom of the river. Had the body not snagged the boom of a passing barge, the child's grave would not have been discovered.

Was it her father? Certainly not. Feckless and foolish, yes, but he loved Georgina and had been making arrangements for her to spend Christmas with him at Mrs Maidment's. In any case, on the day of the murder there is no doubt that he was at his workplace in Spring Gardens.

Was it a purely random killing? Did some woman just select a child, catch a train and then walk her five miles around remote country lanes in the dark before killing her? And did this selfsame random killer just by chance hit upon Yalding, where the lover of the child's father had such close connections? This, too, is quite beyond the bounds of likelihood.

Or Moore's other women? Was it one of them? Surely not. And in any case, would Georgina have gone off with a complete stranger? Would she not, certainly by the time she arrived in Paddock Wood, be distressed to find herself in a strange place with someone she did not know? Yet she had shown no signs of anxiety.

So was it Esther? She had loved the child, taken her out, played with her, bought her toys. But then someone in court recalled her saying, shortly after Georgina disappeared, 'I'm sorry for Mrs Moore but it serves him damned right.'

So was it Esther Pay? Could it really have been her after all? Seeking revenge?

3

THE BALTIC
SAW MILLS MURDER

The murder of Bensley Lawrence at Tunbridge Wells,
July 1888

It was not just the mystery of who had committed the Baltic Saw Mills murder; nor was it simply the seeming absence of motive. It was the manner of the crime, the way in which it was carried out that was so baffling. And why had such an ordinary, harmless sort of man like Bensley Cyrus Lawrence been chosen for what really resembled nothing so much as a street execution? For months after the murder on Friday 20th July 1888, the police at Tunbridge Wells never came near to solving the complexities of the case.

Lawrence had a caller at his back door some time after 9.30 on the night of his death. He was told by his visitor that Mr Potter, foreman at the saw mill next door, wanted him. So Lawrence, the engine man, put on his boots, no doubt grumbling about having to go out on work matters at that time of night, and went with the stranger down the enclosed passageway which led from his house in Mercer Street to Goods Station Road. Only a few yards more and he was at the Baltic Saw Mills. But Mr Potter was not there.

Perhaps Lawrence was not totally unaccustomed to being called out by the foreman; perhaps that is why he went with his visitor without much hesitation. As engine man at the mill he had a responsible job. But it was not an engine room matter that night. What then could Potter want, Lawrence must have asked himself. And why send someone in advance? Why keep him waiting? For Lawrence and the stranger waited in Goods Station Road for about an hour.

Several witnesses were to say that they saw the two men standing outside the saw mill. Frederick Kemp, to whom Lawrence had said goodnight, heard him say, 'Where's Mr Potter? Where's he got to?'

Two men taking their horse-drawn vans into the station yard noticed Lawrence and his companion. Having stabled their horses, they saw them again when they left. From Busby's Coffee House over the road from the mill, yet another witness testified to seeing the men standing in Goods Station Road.

Then, at 10.40, there was a gunshot. Mrs Dennis, passing by shortly afterwards, thought it was a drunk lying there, just inside the timber yard. But then she saw two men lifting Lawrence up and staggering across the road with him to his home.

Once in the house the seriousness of his injury became clear. Lawrence had been shot just in front of the left ear. The doctor at the General Hospital where the wounded man was transferred, noted that the gun had been fired at close range. The skin and hair around the wound were scorched. Lawrence died the next day without gaining consciousness.

Police took statements from neighbours, passers-by, workmates and the usual assortment of dubious local characters. Nothing emerged from their enquiries. No one could identify who had called for Lawrence and stood in the road with him for nearly an hour. Why had the killer waited so long? Was he ensuring that the coast was clear before shooting? Or could he have been plucking up courage?

Even Bertie Lawrence, the dead man's 15 year old son, who had been sent by his mother to see why her husband was away so long, could offer no help. Bertie had spoken to his father who had sent him back home for some matches. Mr Potter, he thought, might want to go into the office and if so, they would need to light the oil lamps. When he returned with the matches, Bertie still did not get a good look at his father's companion.

A couple of youths, hanging around the timber yard before 9.30, reported something unusual. When two strangers had come into the yard, the boys had hidden. They knew they should not be there. But something about the newcomers' demeanour interested them. One of the youths, Helmsley, got within five yards of them. Although he did not recognise them as it was getting dark, he heard a snatch of conversation.

'Now is your time,' one said. 'Be careful what you do.' Then the strangers had parted, both leaving the yard.

What the boys were later to recall is that both wore bowler hats and working jackets. One appeared to be wearing dark trousers and the other corduroys. They said they thought one was about 5ft 10ins and perhaps about 25 years old. Interesting though this information was, it did not advance the police enquiries. The investigation ground to a halt.

Meanwhile other matters grabbed the public imagination at this time; Tunbridge Wells' home-grown murder fell from prominence. Instead there were the mind-numbing Whitechapel Murders. The *Advertiser* even published letters, purportedly from 'The Ripper'.

Then came a letter to the *Advertiser* signed 'Another Whitechapel Murderer' but relating to the Baltic Saw Mills murder. This letter, with its surprising knowledge of what had occurred and its obvious bravado, its cocking a snook at the police, reminded Tunbridge Wells of the murder within its walls.

'Bang!' the letter read, 'and once more Tunbridge Wells was startled with another mystery which is never likely to be found out.' Whilst it did not benefit their investigation, the police had had it confirmed that the murderer was still in their midst.

A young boy had been given the letter to take to the *Advertiser* office. He had been standing in Mount Pleasant Road and a young man had come up to him and asked him to deliver it. Yes, the boy said, he remembered what he looked like. He would be able to recognise him in an identity parade. But even this did not lead directly to the solution the police sought.

On 11th October, at a prayer meeting at the Salvation Army citadel, Captain Cotterill was concluding his sermon, 'Victories and their Cost', when he implored any among the congregation who felt the need, to come up to the penitent bench. Let them in silence tell the Lord of their awful offences, let them come up to be saved. Only two ventured forward, kneeling, praying, silently confessing, asking forgiveness.

Early the following morning William Gower, one of the two young men who had knelt at the penitent bench, turned up at the Captain's house. He was troubled, anxious, the Captain could tell.

'Did you get victory last night?' the Captain asked.

'No,' Gower said, 'I believe my mate got saved and I have come to get saved this morning.'

Captain Cotterill, despite the early hour, must have accounted this a small triumph. After all, if Charles Dobell had been saved last night and Gower had come today to seek salvation, it must have been an effective sermon.

But try as he would that early morning, Gower somehow could not come to God. He and the Army officer discussed the difficulties of seeking salvation, of casting off sin. Did he have anything on his mind, the Captain asked? Gower admitted that he had. The Captain gently urged him to get things off his chest.

The confession came out slowly. It took an hour for the full tale. Since the previous October, Gower said, he and Dobell had been responsible for a lot of bad things. They had set fire to at least half a dozen empty houses; they had fired furze on the common. They were behind everything bad in Tunbridge Wells, Gower told Cotterill.

But the Captain was unprepared for Gower's most startling admission: 'We were at the bottom of the Baltic Saw Mills murder.'

Drunkenness, acts of dishonesty, fornication, wife-beating – that is what the Captain was used to hearing about, that is what those who confessed were most often guilty of.

'Me and my mate did it,' Gower, who worked at the mill as a moulder, went on. 'We tossed up to see who should do it and the lot fell to my mate. We did it out of spite or revenge. Lawrence was a master's man.'

Cotterill was in a quandary. He needed to think, to take advice from his superiors, from people not so closely involved as he had become. And what if he remained silent? There were complex ethical considerations here.

Were they sorry for what they had done, the Captain asked. He must have been disappointed with the reply: 'Well, sometimes we feel if he was to rise up again, we would do it again.'

In the course of the morning Gower sent a letter to Dobell, though where it was written and how it was delivered is unclear.

'My dear mate,' Gower wrote, 'the Holy Ghost entered your heart last night. God only knows I wish it had mine. There seems to be something I could not give up. I went to the Captain this morning and confessed all to him. He wants to see us both tonight at six o'clock. I have not said anything to mother yet.'

As it turned out, Gower and Dobell did not meet Captain Cotterill at six o'clock. Having consulted his district officer, Cotterill went to Superintendent Ebery of Tunbridge Wells police to tell him what he had heard that morning.

Along with other employees of the saw mill, Gower had certainly been questioned earlier and had provided an alibi. The Superintendent looked up the statement. Gower had claimed to be in Frant Road at nine o'clock and in bed by ten. The statement had been marked 'Satisfactory'.

In the afternoon, the Superintendent went with Captain Cotterill to the saw mill. When he saw them Gower shook hands with the Captain, greeting him with the words, 'Well, I thought you would have waited till night.' He was clearly disappointed to see the policeman there.

Potter, the foreman whose name had been used to lure Lawrence from his house, was astounded. 'Dobell had nothing to do with the mill,' he said when the name was mentioned to him. 'What grudge could he have against Lawrence?'

Gower would provide the answer. 'He is a mate of mine,' he told Superintendent Ebery, 'and as true as steel.' It was a matter of loyalty, it seems.

On their way to the police station Gower asked Cotterill's advice. What should he do, he asked. The Captain recommended him to 'out with the lot'.

So the Superintendent heard how the two of them had stood in the timber yard finalising the plan, just as the youth Helmsley had described. Gower indicated, too, where the murder weapon was to be found. It was hidden in a rabbit hutch in an outhouse at 34 Stanley Road, his home, only a few hundred yards from the mill.

The police found a nickel-plated revolver, somewhat neglected, which had been bought for about four shillings. Gower had paid for it himself: Dobell, a plumber, had been frequently out of work that summer and could not afford to pay his share. The pistol had been bought for 'a spree': most of the fictional heroes in the papers and magazines they read had guns.

That evening Dobell was arrested. At first he denied all knowledge of the offence but when he heard that Gower was at the police station, he told Sergeant Bennett: 'You are right. You have got the murderer.'

The news of the arrests astounded Tunbridge Wells. Gower was 18 years old; his mate, Dobell, 17.

Apparently, Gower had come to hate Lawrence who in addition to being the engine man was the timber yard time-keeper. Between September 1886 and July 1888 Gower had been late 27 times. Each time, in accordance with company policy, he was fined a penny. Lawrence had also insulted him by calling him 'a fathead' over some minor matter at work.

In effect, Bensley Lawrence, 'a master's man', died for 2s 3d and what Gower conceived to be an insult. It was a dreadful price to pay.

31

The murder at Tunbridge Wells as illustrated in the press.

The plan was hatched in those summer evenings, probably just days before it was carried into effect, because in the month of July Gower had arrived late at work on six occasions and his resentment was fierce.

But what did Dobell feel? He did not know Lawrence. Yet it was he who called for the man; he who fired the shot when Gower was already at home, in bed, as his statement said. He shot Lawrence out of loyalty to his 'chum'.

The two-day trial of Gower and Dobell opened at Maidstone on 13th December 1888, in front of Mr Justice Mathew who referred to the 'all-absorbing interest of the case which had exceeded that of any capital trial of recent times'.

It certainly was a remarkable case, one which it is unlikely would have been solved but for Gower's confession. But then, perhaps, Dobell might have felt a compulsion to confess. Certainly both boys were obsessed with the murder. Dobell had sent the letter to the *Advertiser* and in October he had bragged to a workmate that he had shot a man. That time he was thought to be joking but perhaps later he might have boasted to someone who took him seriously.

The prosecution argued that the two boys were equally responsible. It did not matter whose finger was on the trigger. One of them committed the crime but he had been heavily influenced by his friend.

Gower's counsel, Mr C. H. Richards, argued that as his client was not present there was no case against him. The Salvation Army had much to answer for, Richards claimed, in working on people's emotions, exciting them to the degree that an impressionable young man confessed to a crime for which he was not responsible. Then, without reflection, simply delighted to have caught another soul, off went the Army officer to the police. Richards mentioned too the boy's respectable family, 'not of the class that would be called the worst characters in Tunbridge Wells'.

In closing, Richards' plea to the jury contained echoes of the Prayer Book which he must have felt appropriate to the case. 'Theirs was an awful responsibility,' the *Courier* reported him as saying, 'and may He to whom all hearts are open and from whom no secrets are hid, help them to arrive at a just conclusion.'

For Dobell, Mr C. F. Gill argued that there was no evidence that he had shot Lawrence. He had undoubtedly sent the letter to the *Advertiser*: the boy whom he had asked to deliver it had identified him. But the letter was just to make a stir, it was not an admission of guilt. As for the boast to his fellow workmates that he had shot a man, that was indicative of some mental imbalance. Dobell had been disturbed by the Salvation Army, 'whose dress, whose mode of worship, their music, their processions, their style, their services, were sensational'.

None of it was any good, the case against them was too strong. The jury was out for only 20 minutes. They recommended mercy.

In Maidstone Gaol, the two young men received an unprecedented flood of visitors, religious and philanthropic, until in the end their numbers had to be restricted. There were petitions for mercy and certainly Gower was confident that he would be reprieved, promising that if he were he would become a Salvation Army preacher.

All in vain. William Gower, 18, and Charles Joseph Dobell, 17, were hanged at the beginning of the year, 1889, at Maidstone Gaol.

4

AN UNQUENCHABLE
DESIRE FOR MONEY

The murder of Bessie Mundy at Herne Bay,
July 1912

Such a summer, day after day of temperatures in the eighties. On the seafront, men in striped blazers and straw boaters; women in long, pastel-coloured muslin dresses carrying parasols. Small boys in sailor suits and little girls in stiff and starchy frocks play with hoops and make sand castles or watch Punch and Judy and the brass bands. There are shows and plays here at Herne Bay; at the cinema, grainy actors in flat white make-up mouth their lines

Herne Bay in 1912, where Smith and Bessie Mundy strolled.

George Joseph Smith and Bessie Mundy.

soundlessly. It seems that this glorious season will never end, that the happiness and innocence of the summer of 1912 will go on for ever.

No doubt Bessie, clutching at Henry's arm, must have hoped that as they strolled along the pier or on the seafront. If only he would always be here, her Henry. Once, he had gone away and had been missing for two years. But then he had come back and found her and she straightaway forgave him. She never wanted to lose him again.

But there is something on Henry Williams' mind. He cannot be totally absorbed by the pleasures and excitements of Herne Bay. He has a money problem and he has to resolve it. As he always has done.

Whether under the name of Williams. Or Love. Or James, Baker, Lloyd. Or other names we do not know. Or even under his own name: George Joseph Smith – the 'Bluebeard of the Bath' as he came to be called.

*   *   *

Bessie Mundy had first met George Joseph Smith two years earlier in 1910 – not that she was ever to know him by that name. Within hours the 33 year old spinster was captivated by him and within days they were engaged. She was overjoyed. She had thought she had been left on the shelf.

Smith, too, was pleased. Bessie had a weekly income of £8 and an emergency sum of £134 she could call on when she wished. There was also £2,500 in gilt edged securities tied up in a trust fund managed by her brother and her uncle.

It is remarkable how Bessie Mundy, genteel middle-class through and through, fell for the working-class ex-convict Smith. But he was already a practised deceiver of women. By the time he met Bessie he had certainly contracted three marriages and possibly more. Several other women had lost their life savings to him. Once the money was in his hands, he simply disappeared from their lives.

This is what happened to Bessie. They married within weeks on 26th August 1910; he prised the £134 from her and, when he realised he could not break into the trust fund, he deserted her on 13th September. All he left her was a note suggesting that she had given him venereal disease. What a shock for a decent, modest woman to be told that.

This was Smith's pattern – pay court, get money, go. 'I feel it a mercy I am rid of him,' the heartbroken Bessie wrote at the time to her brother. 'I feel I am disgraced for life.'

In the meantime the bigamous Smith rejoined another of his wives, the trusting and innocent Edith Pegler. He was now able to resolve his money problems which related to 22 Glenmore Road in Southend, a house he had purchased after an earlier conquest.

Over the next couple of years Smith, a poor businessman, opened and closed antiques and general dealer shops in Southend and Walthamstow. In the spring of 1912, leaving Edith in charge of a shop in Bristol, he went off again, explaining that he would be buying and selling.

On 14th March Smith was in Weston-super-Mare and here he met Bessie Mundy again. It is said that this was a chance meeting but that is unlikely. Smith was a predator, a schemer. He had not forgotten the £2,500 in the trust fund. He somehow knew where to find Bessie and the golden egg. This time he was determined that he would have the money off her.

And the response of the woman he had so shamelessly deserted? Within three hours she had forgiven him, had swallowed whatever tale he told her and had visited a solicitor where Smith signed a document agreeing to repay the £134 'loan' at four per cent. After they had collected Bessie's luggage from the boarding house where she was staying, off they went, the very image of a happy couple.

Soon, however, Smith was being pressed for money by the Woolwich Building Society relating once again to the Southend house. If he had been able to get his hands on the trust fund money straightaway, matters might have turned out differently for Bessie. In the end, however, the only solution was for them to make wills in each other's favour. Murder was the only way out now.

In May, 'Mr and Mrs Williams' arrived in Herne Bay via Woolwich, Ramsgate and Ashford. Smith leased a house, 80 The High Street, for £18 per annum, but careful as ever with his money, he paid for only two months in advance.

80 The High Street was a two storey house with three rooms upstairs and three down. It had no bathroom. This rather suggests that when he first signed the lease he either had not decided to murder Bessie or had not planned to murder her in the way he was to do so. This was – as far as is known – his first murder.

At a hardware shop he found a zinc bath, 'a bare structure on four legs'. He took it on approval, and agreed that if satisfied with it he would pay 37s 6d, having beaten down the price from £2.

There were inconveniences with the bath, of course. He put it in one of the upper rooms and to fill it the hot water had to be carried up from the kitchen. It took about 20 journeys to fill the bath. It took time to heat the water. It was tiring and time-consuming, carrying bucket after bucket. Perhaps the Coroner when he came to consider the drowning of Bessie Mundy ought to have questioned Smith's account more carefully.

On 10th July, Smith took Bessie to young Dr French. His wife had had a fit the previous day, he said. The doctor saw no reason to doubt this. Nor did Bessie. Henry had told her she had had a fit, therefore she must have had.

In the early hours of 12th July, Dr French was called out to see Bessie. She had had another fit whilst she was asleep, her husband said.

Later in the day, Bessie wrote to her uncle telling him of her health problems. 'My husband has been extremely kind,' she wrote, 'and has done all he could for me ... I have made out my will and left all I have to my husband. That is only natural as I love my husband.'

Does this sound natural? Was it dictated? Was Bessie so pathetically naive? Did Smith possess heightened powers of persuasion? Perhaps she was weak; certainly there is no doubt that he could easily bend women to his will.

On Saturday 13th July, shortly after eight o'clock in the morning, Dr French received a brusque note: 'Can you come at once? I am afraid my wife is dead.'

The doctor found Bessie in the bath, facing upwards, her legs over the edge, her head still partially submerged, her right hand clutching a bar of soap.

Epilepsy, Dr French concluded, not asking why the woman's head was still in the water, how she had drowned in such a small bath, why when suffering an epileptic fit she had not relaxed her grip on the soap.

Nor did PC Kitchingham suspect anything when he took the poor husband's statement. Smith had risen at 7.30 am and had gone out for some fresh fish. On his return at eight o'clock, he had found Bessie dead. He had not pulled her out, he said. She was too heavy.

In the afternoon Mrs Millgate, who had been asked to do the laying-out, found Bessie's naked corpse lying on a sheet on the floor. Even after six hours no attempt had been made to preserve the modesty of this decent, trusting woman.

On Sunday, George Mundy received a telegram informing him of his sister's death. His letters to Smith and the Coroner asking for a post mortem arrived too late.

At the inquest on the Monday no one asked how Bessie, in her husband's absence and the space of half an hour, had managed to heat enough water for the bath and to make about 20 journeys up and downstairs with the bucket. Remarkably, a verdict of misadventure was reached.

This was a busy day for Smith. He returned the bath to the hardware shop. He went to the undertaker, arranging for Bessie to be put in an unmarked grave and asking for the funeral to be 'moderately carried out at the cost of seven guineas'. In the evening, he wrote briefly to George Mundy, informing him of the verdict and telling him of the funeral arrangements for the next day. 'I am naturally too sad to write any more today,' he concluded.

On the day of the funeral Smith went to pay off the outstanding instalment of the rent. Although in tears when explaining his wife's death to the secretary, Carrie Rapley, Smith did observe, 'Was it not a jolly good job I got her to make a will?'

Carrie Rapley was to remember that revelation. She remembered, too, how she had asked Smith if he had informed his wife's relatives.

'Yes, I did,' he replied, 'and the brutes sent a letter to the Coroner saying it was a suspicious case.'

By the end of July, Smith was off to Margate to meet Edith Pegler once more. He told her he had been to Canada and she believed him. They moved to Tunbridge Wells, finally leaving Kent in September.

Despite some opposition from Bessie's relatives, most of the money was in Smith's hands by the end of August. The rest was his the following year. With his new wealth he bought seven houses in Bath and took out an annuity. By this time he had accounts in a variety of names in banks all over the West Country and in London. If we wonder what drove Smith, it was an unquenchable desire for money.

By October 1913 Smith felt the need to top up his savings again and once more took leave of Edith Pegler. At Southsea he met Alice Burnham.

On 3rd November, the day before they were married, Smith insured Alice for £500. She died in a bath in Blackpool on 11th November. A week later Smith had sold her belongings, collected the insurance, increased his annuity and moved on. Alice was buried in the cheapest possible coffin. 'After all,' as Smith told the undertaker, 'when they are dead, they are done.'

On 17th September 1914, Alice Reavil, a domestic servant, married Smith. This time he was Charles Oliver James. He left her – alive – on

Sir Bernard Spilsbury.

22nd September. 'What he had taken,' Alice said, 'consisted of the whole of my life savings.'

Later in 1914, as John Lloyd, Smith met Margaret Lofty, a clergyman's daughter. She had only £19 in the bank but he insured her for £700. They married and took rooms in Highgate on 17th December. The following day Margaret Lofty died in the bath. At about the time of her death her husband was heard playing the harmonium and singing *Nearer my God to Thee*. With the proceeds from this particular enterprise, he took out another annuity.

Unfortunately for Smith, a headline in the *News of the World* – 'Bride's Tragic Fate' – alerted Alice Burnham's father. Charles Burnham had once met Smith and had deeply mistrusted him. He straightaway contacted the police who made enquiries. In February 1915, Smith was arrested and charged with bigamy. He was later charged with the murder of Bessie Mundy.

The case was heard at the Old Bailey in June 1915. It vied for newspaper space with clashes of arms, machine guns, death rolls, grenades, dawn raids, courage, horror. And it is a case which still fascinates: 'Brides-in-the-Bath Smith', murderer of at least three women, still grips the imagination.

Some questions are always raised in connection with George Joseph

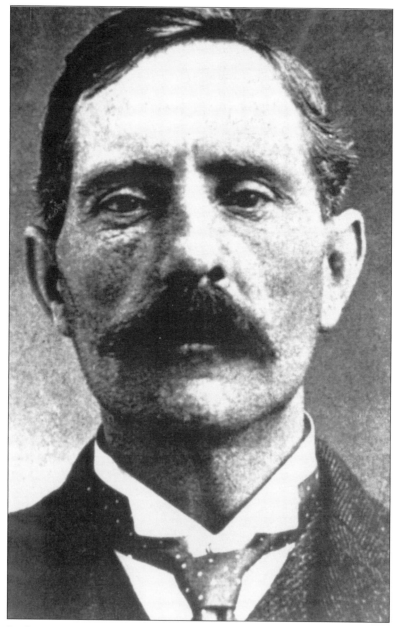

A police photo of Smith, taken at Brixton police station on his arrest.

Smith. The first is how had he drowned his brides? In such small baths, how was this possible?

Sir Bernard Spilsbury, the Home Office pathologist, explained at the trial that it was not possible to drown anyone in these baths simply by pushing them down. They would struggle, hang onto the bath, successfully resist. Spilsbury's experiments with policewomen wearing bathing suits showed exactly how Smith did his work. Standing at the foot of the bath, he grabbed his victims by the back of the knees and tipped them backwards. Simple. Once in the water they were immediately unconscious, instantly drowned.

Another question is how Smith, this systematic bigamist, poorly educated, not terribly prepossessing, managed to persuade women in double-quick time to hand over their money, in some cases their virginity, their very lives? Why did they so quickly agree to marry a virtual stranger, to be insured by someone they knew so little about?

In part, it was because he chose the right kinds of women. They were frequently desperate for a lover, anxious not to be left alone. And he was persuasive, able to convince doctors, solicitors, bank managers, house agents. If he could deal with them, he could deal with unattached and inexperienced spinsters.

Sir Edward Marshall Hall, his defence counsel, had no doubt that Smith hypnotised his prey. One of his victims had spoken of his eyes 'which robbed you of your will'.

After a nine day trial, the jury took only 24 minutes to find him guilty of the murder of Bessie Mundy. George Joseph Smith was hanged at Maidstone Gaol on 13th August 1915.

5

A
FRUSTRATED LOVER

The murder of Sarah Brockman at Ramsgate,
February 1914

Alice Brockman waited on the step
for her mother to answer the door. Why was it locked? It was usually off
the latch. It was only a quarter past eight after all. She peered in the
windows of the modest little house. No sign of life. She couldn't go on
waiting here in the chilly winter night air. She was losing patience. One
more unanswered knock and it was obvious that 24 Seafield Road was
empty. Her mother must have gone out. Alice would have to go round
the back, let herself in that way. She had no anxieties. Southwood was
a quiet enough part of Ramsgate. But to escape the cold night, she
hurried to the back and opened the kitchen door. 'Mother,' she called,
just in case she should be inside this unlit house.

Later in court Alice Brockman, a 25 year old laundry worker, was to
describe what happened to her the night of 18th February 1914.

As soon she entered the kitchen, 'someone sprang from the door and
knocked me down. I did not see who it was. He put a paraffin rag in my
mouth and tied a red rag and a white rag over my face. He tied my
hands behind me and put a pillow over my face. He sat on my knees,
held one hand on the pillow and lit a lamp with the other.'

It was a matter of fact account. It gave no sense of Alice's struggles,
twisting and jerking her body to be free of her attacker; there was no
description of how she kicked out at the man who had punched her to
the ground; nothing was said of how she must have shaken her head
from side to side to stop the rags being tied around her head; nothing of
how she must have bitten the man's hands to stop him forcing the
paraffin rag into her mouth. At the last, despite her struggles, once he

44

had mastered her, tied her wrists with rope, pushed the pillow over her face, he sat on her and almost casually reached over to the oil lamp, removed its glass chimney, took the matches out of his pocket, lit the wick and turned up the lamp. What now, she must have wondered.

'He then put the pillow on one side,' Alice continued, 'and I saw who it was. I said, "Good gracious, Will, I did not think it was you".'

It sounds so calm, this statement. Did she really express her amazement in such terms? Could she anyway, gagged as she was, do more than mumble her surprise, her horrified shock, to see that her assailant was Will Pitcher, the 19 year old with whom she had been walking out for the last two years? They had even spoken of marriage. Recently, of course, Will had been sulking, jealous. Her mother had expressed her disapproval of him only days earlier. And when Alice had told him, he had threatened her. But this attack: it was monstrous.

'He then pulled me up by the rope tied to my hands. I asked him where my mother was and he said, "She has gone down Addington Street." He then said, "You must come upstairs." I then said, "I will not."'

Another version of this scene gives perhaps a closer approximation to Alice's reply. 'I'm not a-going to,' she muttered through her gag when he ordered her upstairs.

We must imagine her struggles now as Pitcher pulled her through the kitchen and into the passageway. She resisted, sobbing and fearful, but he threatened her.

'He said, "If you do not, I will murder you." He pulled me upstairs, carrying the lamp in his hand, threw me onto the bed and assaulted me.'

Desperate now, Alice thought of escape, perhaps wondering if she ever would be free to live. She told him that her brother Fred was due in but even that did not deter young Pitcher. And her mother, had she really gone down Addington Street as he had said? Had something happened to her? Where was she, Alice asked him again? Asleep, he answered.

Now, Pitcher led her downstairs. Here he took off some stockings he had earlier put over his boots, presumably so that when waiting for Alice he could walk silently about the house. And then at last he told her: he had murdered her mother.

'I did not say anything. He took me up and showed her to me and said, "There is your mother."' The frail body of 63 year old Sarah Brockman lay on the bed.

Almost at once, Pitcher led Alice downstairs again. He put on his overcoat and hat and lit a cigarette. Such banal behaviour so frequently surrounds the most dreadful of deeds. And then came the most outrageous of requests.

'He then asked me if I would run away with him. He said he had not got any money and I told him that I had not got any. I was very much terrified and as soon as I could get away from him I rushed out of the back door as he unlocked the front one.' Alice ran to the house next door, rattling the knocker and calling out for help.

She heard Will Pitcher calling out 'Goodnight' to her before he disappeared into the dark.

It was now 9.30 pm and the young woman's ordeal had lasted over an hour. The neighbours to whom Alice had run called the doctor and the police.

When Dr Dunwoody came, he found Sarah Brockman in the room next to that to which Pitcher had taken Alice. The body lay at the foot of the bed, wrists bound behind the back, knees and legs hanging over the end. Only the upper part of the face was visible, the rest was bound with rags and a green scarf. Stuffed in the mouth was a piece of apron, twelve inches long. Blood issued from a single, savage blow to the head although this was not the cause of death. Mrs Brockman had suffocated.

At the post mortem he conducted the following day, the doctor estimated the time of death at about eight o'clock. It is not improbable, therefore, that as Alice tried the front door, looked in the window, came in at the back and struggled in the kitchen, her mother was still alive.

There was no sign of disorder in the room where Sarah Brockman lay. Downstairs, however, in the kitchen there was a pool of blood. In the front room lay a broken chair, the bloodstained trimming of a hat attached to it.

Chief Inspector Paine and a constable from the Ramsgate Borough Police later arrived by taxi at Seafield Road. Whilst Paine studied the scene of the crime, PC Champion, waiting outside the house, was approached by a young man.

'Has anything serious happened here?' the stranger asked. 'I said, "Why?"' PC Champion later told the court.

'And he said, "I am the one you want."

'I said, "What for?"

'He said, "For killing the old woman at 24."

'I said, "Do you know what you are talking about?"

The funeral cortege of Mrs Brockman. (*East Kent Times*)

'He replied, "Yes. That is right. I done it."

'I said, "On your own statement I shall take you to Chief Inspector Paine, the officer investigating this crime."

'He said, "All right. Don't take hold of me. We don't want to cause a scene." '

Champion took Pitcher into the house. The young man, he noticed, seemed very cool. The constable explained to his senior officer what he had been told and Paine began to caution Pitcher. He had not got far when Pitcher interrupted him. 'There is nothing more to say,' he said. 'I am guilty.'

Pitcher looked at the pictures on the wall. He had made the frames for some of them for Alice's mother. 'I do not suppose I shall make any more of them for her,' he said.

The trial of 19 year old William Hearne Pitcher took place at Maidstone on 24th June 1914. The judge was Sir Charles John Darling. Theobald Mathew and Patrick Hastings appeared for the prosecution and Thorn Drury for the defence.

During the whole progress of the trial, which lasted only two and a half hours, Pitcher sat leaning forward with his head almost invisible below the level of the dock. He buried his face in his hands, though for the most part he seemed indifferent to the evidence. Just occasionally he burst into tears.

There was no attempt to argue for his innocence on the part of the defence. The case hinged on whether or not Pitcher was responsible

Sir Patrick Hastings led the prosecution.

for his actions. It all depended on whether he understood the nature and quality of the crime. If he did not, Drury argued, then Pitcher was, at the material time, guilty but insane. It was not a premeditated offence. After all, Pitcher had taken nothing with him with which to tie up Mrs Brockman. The rags, the pillow, the rope, all belonged to the house. 'This', Drury announced, 'is an unhappy story from beginning to end.'

Some days earlier, Alice had told Pitcher that her mother did not like her going out with him. Perhaps she thought him too young or too immature; perhaps the fact that he was out of work counted against him. But what a blow this must have been after a two-year courtship. And after all, he had in the past got on well with Alice's mother. Or at least, he thought he had. Some months earlier he had lodged at 24 Seafield Road for eight weeks or so. He had made the picture frames for Mrs Brockman. And now, the old woman had decided for some reason or other that he was not good enough for her daughter.

When he heard this, Pitcher had responded angrily. 'No one else shall have you or I shall murder you,' he had told Alice several times.

During this same period it might be that Pitcher was having doubts about the sincerity of Alice's feelings towards him. He had become jealous and possessive, perhaps with good reason. Although on Tuesday, 17th February, the day before the murder, he and Alice had been out together and had parted on good terms, can it have been that he suspected that she was seeing another young man? She had in fact put off going out with him on the night of the murder for precisely this reason. Certainly, he had recently taken to hanging about the outside of the house after he had seen Alice home in the evening. Did he suspect, was he right to suspect, that once he was out of sight, she might go out and meet some rival?

Pitcher's account of the murder was that he went to see Mrs Brockman to talk matters over, to get her to see him in a better light. Mrs Brockman had let him into the house sometime after 7.30 pm when she had come back from a brief shopping expedition. But the discussion did not take the turn he had intended. By the time Alice came home at a quarter past eight, her mother was already lying on the bed upstairs, her wrists tied, her mouth gagged, her skull bloody from a savage blow and dying or already dead.

In defending his client, Mr Drury admitted that Pitcher had murdered Sarah Brockman but claimed that at the time of the attack he was not responsible for his actions. Pitcher committed the murder, according to counsel, because that was his nature. Normally, he was an apathetic young man but given to uncontrollable outbursts. But then, Drury pointed out, there was insanity in the family. Six members on his father's side were in asylums.

An uncle, John Clayson, took the stand. He sometimes thought Will not of sound mind. 'I have questioned him about it and he has said "I can't help it, uncle."'

A former employer, Alfred Grummant, a builder, had had to talk to the accused about this temper. 'He simply lost himself when he lost his temper,' he said. And there was the young fellow's emotional immaturity too. Once, after Pitcher had finished a job, Grummant had told him to go up to the shop to clear away shavings, 'whereupon he sat down in the office and commenced to cry, saying, "I cannot go up there for the boys laugh at me."'

Drury also teased evidence out of Chief Inspector Paine about a curious case which occurred just before Christmas 1913. One of Pitcher's sisters, a 15 year old, was in service. One evening her master and mistress had gone out, leaving her in charge of the baby. When the owners returned they found the girl lying unconscious in the passage. Chief Inspector Paine told the court, 'I called at the house at which she was employed as a servant in consequence of a complaint being made to me and she then made a statement to me. She had been assaulted in her master's house while alone there and had been tied up and gagged.' There had been no robbery.

'She gave me a description of a man but I was unable to connect any man with the description she gave me.' It seems to have been rather vague although the assailant was said to be a young man who spoke 'better than ordinary'.

It is a curious tale. Was it Pitcher? He is unlikely to have spoken 'better than ordinary'. In any case, would his sister not have recognised him? Surely she would. Did this assault give Pitcher some idea? Or was this some even more complex occasion?

Drury's reason for mentioning the offence is obvious: he wished to give the impression that his client was insane enough to have attacked his own sister. But the truth of the matter is more elusive.

Dr Hoar, MO at Maidstone Prison, had ample opportunity to observe Pitcher. He believed Pitcher's statement that he had no memory of the attack on Alice and 'that it is quite possible in a case of epileptic mania, in a person of degenerate mind, that he would do that sort of thing. In fact, he ran amok.'

There was no medical evidence to support any notion of epileptic mania. Much was made of the fact, however, that one of Pitcher's sisters was epileptic.

Dr Fitzgerald, Chief Medical Superintendent at Chatham Asylum, expressed his view that at the time of the murder, Pitcher was insane. He was one of those, the doctor opined, who lose control without warning.

The only time that Pitcher showed any life during the trial was when Alice Brockman told the court that he had once smacked her across the mouth. Pitcher was roused. 'He started violently to his feet,' the *East Kent Times* tells us. 'His face was crimson and leaning over the side of the dock, he burst out, "Alice, I have never laid hands on you."'

Even this brief outburst served Drury as an illustration of Pitcher's ungovernable temper although in cold print it does, in the circumstances, seem quite understandable and extremely mild.

The prosecution was quite satisfied not to challenge the central issue of Pitcher's sanity. In the end the jury retired only briefly. Pitcher was found guilty but insane at the time of the offence. He spent the rest of his life in custody as a criminal lunatic.

6

THE SHOOTING AT
STELLA MARIS

The shooting of Jack Derham at Tankerton,
August 1926

According to one of his friends, Frank Smith – Alfonso Francis Austin Smith to give him his name in full – was 'a bit erratic and of a highly volatile disposition', a man 'capable of any silliness'.

It seems to be a judgment not far off the mark. He did after all race through enormous legacies from his father and two grandfathers, each of them a millionaire.

Nor was his prodigality the sole cause of doubt about his temperament. In 1913, when he was 24 years of age, he suddenly resigned his commission in the Guards. At the outbreak of war the following year he enlisted in the Seaforth Highlanders. As a private. Something odd there.

After the war Smith resumed his wayward life, accumulating four bankruptcies and a divorce. By 1925 he had assets of a mere £10,000, an exquisitely beautiful wife and three very young children. Whilst still able to afford a nanny and to lead a not too spartan existence, Smith had reached a point where he seriously began to think of picking up some kind of job at the Stock Exchange.

Before any such drastic step was taken, however, his wife Kathleen had an operation and to help her recuperate in the autumn of 1925, the Smiths took a furnished house at Herne Bay. It was here at a Christmas party they met the dashing Jack Derham, a man in his late thirties and a former ice-hockey international. The two men struck up an immediate friendship. They had, of course, several friends in common, both being Old Etonians and Cambridge graduates.

Kathleen Smith.

For months the Smiths and Derham were constant companions. Derham, separated from his aristocratic wife, was a free agent. He regularly drove across to the Smiths' house, Llangollen, at Herne Bay from his home at nearby Broomfield where he now lived with his mother.

But like so many sudden and intense friendships this one soured. One night in June, the two men had a fist fight in the house, Smith laying out his powerfully built visitor. And the reason? Derham had fallen in love with Kathleen, and she with him.

Smith was desperate. Whatever his faults, he loved his wife and children passionately. Now he feared he would lose them. By the end of June, wretchedly unhappy, he had packed his bags and moved to London. He did some work on commission at the Stock Exchange though how energetically and effectively cannot be said. It was a period during which he drank heavily, his life in disarray.

Back in Kent, Derham and Kathleen met daily and they were by now undoubtedly lovers, although Derham never spent the night at Llangollen.

Smith made one trip home, staying the weekend, but failed to make any headway. Kathleen would not give up Jack Derham. Only a day or so after his return to London, the wretched man received a letter from

Kathleen's solicitor. She wished for a formal separation. Smith sank into yet greater despair.

About this time, in early July, Derham moved to Dollis Hill where he could be near his mother who was in a London hospital. Almost immediately Kathleen and the children moved into Claverhouse, Derham's home at Broomfield. It was a temporary measure. The lease at Llangollen had expired and in a couple of weeks Kathleen was due to move to Stella Maris, another furnished house, at Tankerton near Whitstable. It ought to be emphasised that whilst Kathleen lived at Claverhouse, Derham was away in London. When, however, she went to London one weekend, she stayed at the Dollis Hill house.

In these days Smith was deeply distressed and drinking heavily. These were not the best circumstances for a man of his erratic temperament to find himself in. It may explain his letter to Derham's totally innocent mother in which he wrote, 'No doubt you are aware that your son Jack has seduced my wife.' He warned her that he would obtain satisfaction 'with my own hands'.

A day or so later, on 15th July, Smith turned up at Claverhouse to have it out with Kathleen. She was not there but the children were, with their nanny, Miss Wyatt. Smith took the children for a walk. Later, on his return, Miss Wyatt noticed a change in his mood. He had been drinking. He told her that he intended to kill his wife and Derham, and while she and the children stayed upstairs in a locked bedroom, Smith for a quarter of an hour smashed china, glass and furniture in an orgy of fury. His anger was heightened no doubt by his discovery in the house of letters from Derham to Kathleen.

The following day Smith called at his solicitors. There would be no separation, he raged. These letters constituted grounds for divorce. He went off, threatening to find Derham and 'smash him up'.

But instead of confronting his rival, Smith now began channelling his emotions through letters, trying somewhat ineptly to win back his wife.

'My dear, dear girl,' he wrote to Kathleen, 'this problem can only be solved in one way, the removal of your lover or myself.' Was he threatening suicide? Or murder? Or was he merely making a rational statement of the facts?

Derham, too, was sent a letter. His began 'You damned swine' and went on to tell the 'lily-livered fool' that he would suffer.

At the beginning of August, Smith wrote again to Kathleen. This letter is a mixture of remorse, love and anger. He is so miserable, Smith tells her, he could die. If she comes back to him he will stop drinking. His heart is broken. Then his mood swings. He tells her that he will find 'that damned cad Derham' and deal with him. In fact, he will deal with both of them 'in a fashion that can never be mended'.

Kathleen did not help. She promised to meet him on 6th August at the Grosvenor Hotel but she did not turn up. She had been in London, though: she had met Derham. Smith knew of this and fired off another letter.

'If I do not hear from you by Monday,' he wrote, 'I shall do something desperate.' There was a postscript too: 'God help Derham if he is coming to Tankerton. I have not started on him yet.'

Over the weekend the anguished Smith, brooding in London, visited a friend, a former naval officer. Would he lend him his revolver, Smith asked. And ammunition. Fact was, Smith told him, he was going over to Ireland and needed to protect himself against the Sinn Feiners who had already burnt down some property of his.

All untrue, but on Monday, 9th August, when Smith arrived at Kathleen's new address, Stella Maris at Tankerton, he had a revolver in his pocket. A telegram from Kathleen had invited him down. Clearly she wished in some way to resolve their untidy lives.

The old ground was gone over. His love for her; her betrayal of him; the needs of the children. Would she not give up Derham? At one point, taking out the revolver, Smith threatened suicide. Nevertheless, by the end of the evening they were once more on amicable terms. Before they went to bed – in separate rooms – Smith put the gun out of harm's way in the drawing room coal-box. The next day Kathleen and her 16 year old sister, Lilian Wight, who was also staying at Stella Maris, found the revolver and hid it. It was just possible that Smith might attempt to kill himself.

But Tuesday was a wonderful day. Kathleen at last promised to give up Derham. After all, there were the children to consider and obviously Frank loved her deeply. That night she and her husband slept together. For him, the anguish of recent months was ended. Perhaps she too may temporarily have felt that her anxieties were over.

The next morning Smith wrote a letter to his wife. It began 'My own adorable little wife' and it expressed the depth of his feelings for her. He described himself as like a man who had just recovered from a terrible fever. As Kathleen went off shopping to Herne Bay, he handed her the letter to read on the bus.

But when she returned, Kathleen had changed her mind. She would not, could not, give up Jack Derham. Once more, Smith was plunged into despair; the house was shrill with recriminations.

On Thursday 12th August, Derham received a telegram asking him to come to Stella Maris to discuss matters. It appeared to have been sent by Kathleen. In fact, Smith was the sender. It was his ruse to get his rival to Tankerton.

When Derham arrived that evening the meeting was more civilised than might have been expected. Perhaps Derham and Kathleen knew that the temperamental Smith had to be played low-key.

During the evening Smith asked if he might have back his revolver. He wanted it: he was going to sell it. Not wishing to create a scene, Kathleen handed it to him though only after she had held it and the ammunition under the kitchen tap. When Smith dried his property thoroughly, no one made any comment. How astonishing given the circumstances and the man's volatile temperament.

In the course of their discussions, Smith proposed that he and Derham should go out of Kathleen's life for three months. She would have time to think things over. This was a departure. Perhaps Smith was really trying to prove that he was a reasonable man, truly considerate of his wife's needs.

Less helpfully, Kathleen and Derham proposed that Smith should go out of *their* lives. What about Smith and Kathleen going to Paris? They could divorce cheaply there. Now in a hysterical outburst, Smith took out the revolver, once again threatening suicide, but he was easily disarmed.

Then when all had calmed down, and unlikely as it seems, the three of them went off for supper at the Marine Hotel at Tankerton. Presumably they continued their debate there without any noticeable disturbance.

Sometime during the evening it was suggested that Smith should sleep at the hotel. Outrageous. For the last two nights he and Kathleen had slept together. The matter seems not to have been pursued and all went home together. Back at Stella Maris, however, when he discovered his wife and her sister making up a bed for Derham, Smith was beside himself with rage. 'I won't have this lover of yours sleeping here,' he shouted.

Then all anger once more subsided. When Kathleen and Smith went down to the drawing room, Derham had some playing cards out on the table. Possibly he felt there had been enough unresolved discussion for one day. Or perhaps he was trying to introduce some normality into a fraught household.

Smith, according to his account, was preparing to sit at the table to play. In court, he explained what then occurred: 'It all happened in a flash. I went to get the chair and as I did so I put my hand to unbutton the back pocket of my trousers to take out the revolver.'

'I was getting the chair and pulling out the revolver,' Smith continued. 'All I know is that there was a terrific struggle. I was struck on the head, the revolver went off and the next thing I am absolutely conscious of was speaking to Inspector Rivers.'

Lilian Wight, hearing the shot, ran downstairs from her bedroom to find the drawing room in turmoil. Smith was on the floor, Derham sitting on top of him, raining blows with the revolver butt. Kathleen, screaming 'Don't, don't', was vainly trying to pull her lover away. Eventually, Derham and Smith were separated by the two women.

As the uproar subsided Derham, still carrying the revolver, wandered out of the house and into the street. On the pavement he staggered and fell. No one seems to have realised it but he had been shot in the stomach. An ambulance was called and the gravely injured man taken off to St Helier's Nursing Home.

When Inspector Rivers and Sergeant Quested of the local police arrived they found Smith bruised and bleeding from a gashed head. 'I intended to shoot myself,' he told the Sergeant, 'but in the struggle for the revolver it went off.'

'Have I killed him?' Smith asked later. 'Derham has been carrying on with my wife,' he said at another stage by way of explanation. 'I had no option but to put an end to it.'

'How is he? Where is the seducer?' he asked the Inspector when told that he was to be charged with wounding. There is no coherent admission in these remarks of what Smith's intentions had been. But when Jack Derham died the next day, he was charged with murder.

The trial which opened at Maidstone on 25th November 1926 lasted three days. It was perhaps the most glamorous murder of the decade, its two principals 'a typical army officer' and his wife 'dressed entirely in black and very girlish looking'.

What really mattered in this trial was not the chaotic domestic lives of the three main characters nor even the fact that Smith had threatened Derham several times. The focus was on what precisely occurred in the few seconds prior to the revolver being fired. Had there been a struggle as a result of which the weapon was discharged? Or was the gun fired deliberately before Derham and Kathleen launched themselves at Smith?

Sir Edward Marshall Hall appeared for the defence.

James Barton who had been passing the house at the crucial time offered telling evidence. From the footpath outside the house he had seen Derham standing in the room with Kathleen near him. It was a typical snapshot view of any lit-up room at night. Barton had turned away only to hear a shot almost immediately. As he looked once more towards the window he saw Derham and Kathleen, their arms outstretched, moving towards Smith, pushing him to the ground. As he fell, Smith lurched towards the window, breaking a pane of glass. Then Barton saw Derham raising his fists and appearing to strike someone or something on the floor.

In sum, Barton's evidence was that he heard the shot and saw the fight begin after that.

Sir Edward Marshall Hall, for the defence, put up a bravura performance, one of his last. He painted a portrait of Smith as a victim, a man most cruelly used. And he sought to persuade the jury that Derham, snatching at the gun, had shot himself. The advocate totally overcame the expert witnesses like the gunsmith Robert Churchill whose professional opinion was that no one but Smith could have pulled the trigger.

The judge, Mr Justice Avory, was not impressed by the defence argument. Why, he asked in summing up, had Smith a loaded revolver if he did not intend to use it? Why had he sent a telegram to Derham in his wife's name? And most significant, why had Kathleen not been called for the defence? She could not be asked to testify against her husband but she had seen all that had occurred. Why had the defence not called her? Was it because she was unable to support her husband's account?

The jury withdrew for two hours. When they returned with a not guilty verdict, there were cheers in the courtroom. Outside Kathleen was to face a hostile crowd.

The woman in the case is so often held to be the most guilty party.

Nor was the judge satisfied with the verdict. He observed to Smith, 'The jury has taken upon your trial the most lenient view that was possible in this case ... I have my own opinion on it.'

He then sentenced Smith to twelve months' hard labour on a charge of possessing a firearm with intent to endanger life.

The shooting at Stella Maris was a mystery. In some senses it remains so though many, like Mr Justice Avory, have their own opinion on it.

7

MURDER AT THE
CHINESE LANTERN CAFÉ

The murder of Sonia Ramsay at Broadstairs,
May 1927

'The scarlet Chinese lantern hanging from the gaudily painted ceiling clashed with the black lacquer bowl of gay flowers on the centre table.'

Good colourful stuff this from the *Evening News* reporter. That is probably how the Chinese Lantern Café looked at the time. Then the writer warms to his trade. There has been a murder here: even more colourful stuff is required for his editor. 'She loved all things Oriental and could manipulate men with the greatest of ease.'

When she opened the café only a year or so earlier no doubt Sonia Ramsay intended it to be exotic. As exotic, that is, as Broadstairs in 1926 could bear. Genteel and respectable, it was not the kind of seaside town to favour the garish. But Sonia was a woman of taste, well-connected and not at all likely to overstep the bounds of what was proper. She had been well brought up in India where her father had been in business and where the family was on close terms with the Viceroy. Returned to England, the family was very friendly with Lord Roberts. So Sonia, in opening the café in Harbour Street, is likely to have caused no more than the raising of the odd pained eyebrow.

The café had flair and some elegance. So had Sonia, flitting around the tables in silk Oriental gowns, her hair immaculately styled. She was a striking woman, and whilst she seems to have captivated men, there is no suggestion at any stage that she manipulated them. Indeed, there are compelling indications of her loyalty to her husband whom she had married in her teens when he had just come down from Cambridge and was studying for the Bar. Towards the end of the war, when the last of

Genteel Broadstairs where Sonia Ramsay met her death.

their three children was born, her husband, a Flying Corps pilot, had been permanently crippled in a flying accident. Now, years later, he trusted her enough to encourage her to continue to go dancing in the ballrooms of Margate, Ramsgate and Broadstairs.

Perhaps in Broadstairs that might have raised eyebrows, too – his compliance, her shamelessness is how it might have been construed – but Sonia was lively and somewhat Bohemian. Wasn't her sister a novelist, her critics might have observed. And so harmlessly, now 37, Sonia danced and still managed to be faithful to her husband.

On the morning of 1st June 1927, Sonia's mother, Mrs Heilger, noticed that her daughter had not returned home to the house they shared in Lindenthorpe Road. Sonia had told her the previous day that she would not be in late that evening but even when ten o'clock and then midnight passed, Mrs Heilger had assumed that her daughter was at some friend's house. At nine o'clock the next morning, however, she was uneasy and took herself off to the café.

The front door was locked but Mrs Heilger gained entry through the back. There was no one downstairs. She went upstairs. There, her back hard against the door, Sonia lay dead in one of the rooms.

The police were sent for. Inspector Goldsmith, in charge of the Broadstairs station, came first and was later joined by Superintendent Lane and Detective Sergeant Avery.

Sonia Ramsay. (*Isle of Thanet Gazette* – Margate Library Local Studies Collection)

Sonia Ramsay was fully dressed, wearing a brilliant scarlet Chinese robe, gold dragons embroidered on the back. A white sheet had been draped over her and this concealed the severe blow to her head and the towel round her neck. There was a considerable amount of blood on the floor and on the lower part of the walls. Although the furniture at the other end of the room was undisturbed, it was obvious that a fierce struggle had taken place.

A trail of bloody footsteps led from the room to a bedroom on the opposite side of the stairway. In the cupboard of the washstand the police found a bloodstained hammer. In the fire grate was a pair of men's shoes, their soles caked with dried blood. In the cupboard hung a jacket, a waistcoat and trousers, all of them stained with blood.

And on the dressing table was an eight-page letter confessing to the murder. It was written by Charles Robinson who lived above the café of which he seems to have been – though nothing is certain – a part-owner.

If there is some doubt about his status in the café there was even more ambiguity about his place in the Ramsay household. Almost since the Ramsays had arrived in Broadstairs two or three years earlier, Robinson, separated from his wife, had lived with them, first in a flat and then at the café. He had been appointed to look after Mr Ramsay and he was especially qualified to do this for he was a first-class nurse and a highly-trained masseur. Only recently, however, the Ramsays had gone to live at Mrs Heilger's house in Lindenthorpe Road, leaving Robinson on his own at the café.

This was the man whom the police now sought. Robinson, a fascinating man, 'a most able and entertaining conversationalist', was 54 years old, well-known in the area. He ought not to have been difficult to find. Over the next 24 hours he was reported as having been in a Cliftonville hotel and the next evening he was seen in Northgate Road in Margate.

It was not until Tuesday noon that he was found. A builder's labourer working in a field at Stone House came across the hunted man lying among some shrubs. Had he rolled only a few feet, he would have fallen over the cliff edge.

Robinson was unconscious, his face blue, his tongue swollen and a yellow froth oozed from his mouth. On his left temple there was a bruise; there were abrasions on his knuckles and one eye was discoloured. On the grass beside him was a large medicine bottle containing a yellow liquid, a small aspirin bottle, and a bottle of whisky. There was an incongruity about this man, dying in the bushes, in his formal black jacket and striped trousers, his waistcoat and socks stained with blood. 'But no hat,' the *Isle of Thanet Gazette* observed primly.

The critically ill man was rushed to Ramsgate hospital 'in a motor ambulance'. Nothing could be done for him: he had taken a corrosive poison and died within two hours.

The two inquests – Sonia's at Broadstairs police station and Robinson's at Ramsgate Town Hall – combined to reveal a tale of intense possessiveness and obsessive love. Also revealed was the way in which Robinson, in the two or three years in which he had lived with the Ramsays, had tried and in part had succeeded in imposing his will on them. Mrs Heilger, who for most of that time had not been living with her daughter and son-in-law, had been a fascinated observer of a curiously developing relationship. 'He', said Mrs Heilger referring to

63

The Chinese Lantern Café. (*Isle of Thanet Gazette* – Margate Library Local Studies Collection)

Robinson, 'rather seemed to want to take the part of mentor.' Certainly he had begun to assume the role of head of the house.

Mrs Heilger told how her daughter had for many years lived 'a lonely and rather difficult life because her husband was an invalid'. There must have been some frustrations and temptations for this woman who was so charming, according to her mother, that 'no man could fail to be attracted by her'. At least, Ramsay understood his wife's difficulties and never objected when she went out dancing. 'She lived for dancing,' Mrs Heilger said. 'It was her one great pleasure in life. She danced beautifully and was as light on her feet as a fairy.'

And Robinson, infatuated, began to learn to dance. It was absurd, Sonia's mother said, to see 'an elderly man' like Robinson practising the Charleston. When he asked Sonia if he might accompany her to dances, he was rebuffed. Well, then, he had said, he would turn up at the halls she went to. And Sonia had replied that if he went to one dance, she would go to another.

So now Robinson adopted another tack. He rebuked Sonia for going to so many dances. Increasingly he objected to her dance hall visits. On one occasion she had to call in her husband to remonstrate with Robinson and to tell him that his wife could go out where, when and with whom she pleased.

It was an absurd situation relieved only marginally when the Ramsays left the Chinese Lantern Café. Now, however, on her return home some nights, Sonia felt that she was being followed. One evening in the café, as she was leaving for a dance, Robinson had taken hold of her by the arm. He would not let her go, he said. But she, self-possessed, had laughed, shrugged him off and gone on her way.

And so it must have been on the evening of 31st May 1927. There is some confusion about the time Sonia met her death. It is most likely that she died early in the evening as she was preparing to leave for a dance. She would not have gone to the café on her return: she would not wish to see Robinson at that time of night.

Witnesses at the inquests spoke of Robinson's severe nervous breakdown which had changed his personality. His daughter Constance spoke of him as a loving father who after the breakdown had sudden uncontrollable outbursts of temper. Dr Warwick Brown, who had known and respected Robinson for over 20 years, referred to the breakdown, saying that now he seemed at times to be on the borderline of insanity.

Extracts from letters he had written suggested the man's lack of balance. One letter, which appears to have been composed only a short time after the murder, read: 'I told her a month ago if I found out I would show her no mercy . . . Had this woman only been frank and told me the truth that would have been enough. But it is for her lies and deceit that she has paid the penalty.'

Nowhere is there any evidence of Sonia's 'lies and deceit'. What we have here is a man's delusions. To his wife, Robinson wrote, probably the morning before the murder: 'I am afraid I am going to bring a great deal of pain and trouble on you but it will be the last . . . All through you have been correct in what you have said about Mrs Ramsay. I know now she is the most violent woman on God's earth.'

Questioned about this letter which included unfounded accusations against several people, Dr Brown told the Coroner, 'To me, it is a letter of an insane man, a man with an unhealthy attitude of mind.'

The doctor added that he believed that Robinson was insane when he took a poison which as an experienced nurse he must have known would cause him the most awful agonies.

Oddly enough, the café had been failing. And Sonia seems not to have had enough money to save it. It was perhaps not quite right for sedate Broadstairs. On the day of the murder, the electricity had been cut off.

There was something symbolic in that, perhaps.

8

MOTHER AND SON

The murder of Rosaline Fox at Margate,
October 1929

Devoted sons are admired. They are noticed too, possibly because there are so few of them. And when Sidney Harry Fox arrived at the Metropole Hotel at Margate in that bitterly cold October of 1929, no man could have looked more devoted to his mother, a frail little soul, a semi-invalid, suffering from Parkinson's Disease. Sidney was ever-caring, giving her those little wistful smiles, the occasional sad look. Such a self-sacrificing young man, taking his mother everywhere. Not many 30 year olds would do that.

They had been on the move since March from their home in Norfolk. There had been visits to London and to Cambridge but in recent weeks they had been in Kent. They had stayed in a variety of hotels and boarding houses – the Sun at Chatham, the Grand at Dover among them – and after visiting another son's war grave at Arras, Rosaline Fox and Sidney had stayed in Folkestone and Canterbury. Now they had returned to Margate where in August they had spent some days at a boarding house.

Those who studied Sidney closely might have noticed that though he was always smart, he did not have an extensive wardrobe. He had, in fact, only one suit, regularly brushed and kept clean with dabs of lighter fuel; his raincoat was in pawn. As for the 63 year old Rosaline, she possessed two dresses, a light coat and one pair of shoes. During this cold spell she wore all of her few clothes during the day. In bed, having no nightdress, she wore her vest.

So few clothes and staying at the Metropole? Not even a suitcase?

67

Mrs Rosaline Fox, the victim.

Sidney had explained away the non-arrival of their luggage but hired the hotel safe for a package of what he said were valuables. In fact the package was empty.

Still, for seven months they had lived better than they had previously

68

done. When in March Sidney had been released from his two year sentence for theft, he had immediately gone to St Mary's Hospital in Portsmouth where for two years his mother had been an inmate, classified as a pauper.

Now with only modest means – Rosaline had a 10s a week pension, Sidney an 8s a week service pension – they managed to survive, sometimes abandoning luggage, paying with dud cheques or simply disappearing from their hotels and boarding houses.

Whether Rosaline was fully aware of what was happening is unclear: she was certainly in a frail physical state and possibly equally infirm mentally. It was Sidney who carried it all off, with his public school charm, though he had never been educated beyond village elementary school. He talked of his being of independent means though he was penniless; of a father who owned flour mills though in reality he had worked on the railway. Sidney Harry Fox, who had rarely worked, was very persuasive. He owned a farm, he told them at the Metropole.

When then was the moment he decided to do away with the mother he apparently doted on? Before he retrieved her from the workhouse? In the course of their travels? On that day at the Metropole when he asked if his mother might have a warmer room and they put her in Room 66 which had a gas fire and a connecting door to his room?

Had Sidney now realised that the jaunt could not continue? He was in dire financial straits. But then, when had he not been? His life from childhood had been littered with thefts and frauds and yet he never seemed to be out of debt. And work had rarely presented itself as a solution to his problems.

In the last few months he had skipped off from a Margate boarding house without paying; at the Royal Pavilion at Folkestone which they left on 12th October, he had stolen a cheque book and raised £15 from it before again leaving an unpaid bill; at the County Hotel, Canterbury, where he stayed the next three days, he had paid only £2 of a bill for £4 16s 0d. Immediately before arriving in Margate on 16th October he and Rosaline had enjoyed a meal at the Savoy Restaurant in Dover where he had failed to pay the bill in full. It could not go on.

When Sidney brought his mother out of the workhouse at Portsmouth he had paid off the arrears on a small insurance policy on his mother's life. At the same time, out of gratitude, Rosaline changed her will – not that she had much – leaving all to Sidney. To his brother, who had refused to look after her, she left a farthing.

Over the months of their journey Sidney insured his mother, quite

Sidney Harry Fox.

cheaply, at different times for sums of up to £2,000. On occasions there would be a promised pay-out for injury or disablement, sometimes for death. He dealt with several companies: Eagle Star, Ocean, Royal, Cornhill, Sun. Sometimes the policies were renewed, sometimes they were allowed to lapse. There is no reason to say categorically that he was from the start planning to murder Rosaline. After all, taking out

70

insurance was prudent, especially as his mother was in ill-health.

What is certain is that by 22nd October – that is, within six days of their coming to Margate – Sidney had decided it was time to act. On that day he went to London, like a devoted son leaving one of the hotel staff a generous tip to keep an eye on his mother.

In London, he extended by 36 hours or so a policy with Cornhill Insurance, covering his mother for £2,000 'in the event of violent external death or injury'. This policy had previously been extended several times, usually till noon. This time, it was to expire at midnight on 23rd October. Sidney explained this brief extension by saying that he and his mother would be travelling the next day and his mother worried if, when on a journey, she was not insured. He also took out a one-day policy for £1,000 with Ocean Accident. The Royal and the Sun turned down his proposals. They were, it seems, a shade uneasy.

That night Sidney stayed in London with a male friend – he was bisexual – who lent him £1 with which, thoughtful as ever, he bought flowers and a bottle of port for Rosaline.

At the Metropole on his return next day he told staff how much better his mother was. 'We have had a sham fight which shows she is well,' he told them in his artless, boyish manner. They would be leaving next day, he said, asking for his bill to maintain the pretence. They were off to his farm at Lyndhurst which, he told someone, was being looked after by his steward, 'a capable fellow'.

After he had put his mother to bed he went down to the bar, bought drinks for the hotel band, and then retired for the night at 10.40 pm. He had one hour and 20 minutes before the policy expired.

An hour later, at 11.40 pm, Sidney was raising the alarm, calling out that there was a fire in his mother's room.

'Where's "the boots"? I believe there is a fire,' he was shouting. 'Where's "the boots"? There is a fire and my mother is up there.'

Samuel Hopkins, staying at the Metropole, tied a handkerchief around his face and crawled into the smoke-filled Room 66. He kicked a smouldering armchair into the passageway and dragged out the old lady who was wearing only her vest.

It was too late for Rosaline. She was certified as having died from shock and smoke inhalation. Sidney was distraught. The hotel manager's wife calmed him, held him, stroked the weeping man's head.

Another matter also seemed to be disturbing him. His mother had recently cashed a cheque, he said. 'Has the money been found?' he asked the doctor. 'There was £25 in her handbag. Have they got that?' It was a fiction, of course, and not a wise one in the circumstances.

Learning that there would have to be an inquest he was clearly worried, though at the time his collapse was attributed to shock. At the inquest the following day a verdict of death by misadventure was returned. The old woman had apparently placed her clothes and papers on an armchair next to the gas fire with fatal results.

Now, on the strength of the money due to him, Sidney borrowed £40 from a Margate solicitor and went off to Norfolk to attend his mother's funeral. Characteristically, he left the Metropole without settling his bill, but he did send a letter to the receptionist. 'It doesn't seem only a week ago the poor dear soul was alive,' he wrote. 'How I shall miss her. We were such pals.'

Rosaline was buried in the afternoon of 29th October at Great Fransham. In the morning Sidney had fitted in a visit to the insurance offices in Norwich. He also at this time badgered other branches for payment, but the insurance companies were not totally convinced about Rosaline's death. This business of extending the policy worried them. They contacted the police.

Back in Margate there was also some uneasiness. The manager at the Metropole brooded over the unpaid bill. His wife thought of how she had tried to comfort Sidney on the night of the fire, how she had stroked his head. Why, she wondered, had her hands reeked so much of smoke? She had not entered Room 66. Nor for that matter had Sidney. He had seen the smoke in his mother's room, shut the door and run downstairs for help. So if he had not been in Room 66, how was it that his hair retained a smell of smoke? The manager and his wife discussed their uneasiness, and contacted the police.

Then there was the Margate boarding house landlady with whom Sidney and Rosaline had stayed in August. She saw the story in the newspaper and recognised the old lady and her attentive son. They had not paid their bill, so how could they afford to stay at the Metropole? It sounded very fishy and, in any case, she wanted her money. She too was soon in touch with the police.

In early November, Sidney was arrested and charged with obtaining credit whilst still an undischarged bankrupt. It was enough to hold him whilst Chief Inspector Hanbrook of Scotland Yard waited for Sir Bernard Spilsbury's examination of Rosaline's exhumed body.

Spilsbury concluded that the old lady had not been suffocated by the smoke. There was no soot in her lungs and not a trace of carbon monoxide in the blood. She had been dead before the fire broke out. A small bruise in the soft tissues between the larynx and the oesophagus indicated that she had been strangled.

Sidney Harry Fox was charged with murder. The trial, held at Lewes, began on 12th March 1930 and lasted nine days. Newspapers commented on the accused man's dapper appearance and his calm manner.

The prosecution demolished the suggestion that the fire had been an accident. Fox was alleged to have placed clothes and papers on the chair in front of the fire. These had been burnt. At the same time, he had started a fire with petrol under the chair, adding something which gave off a dense smoke. But there was a give-away: there was a strip of carpet between the gas fire and the chair which showed no signs of burning. It was an amateur bungle.

Most probably Rosaline, who had drunk half the bottle of port her son had bought her, never realised what her devoted son was doing when he placed his hands around her neck.

Mr Cassels, for the defence, had Sidney admit that he was a con-man. The suggestion was that he would draw the line at murder.

Cassels: Did you sometimes leave hotels without paying?

Fox: Yes, sir.

Cassels: Did you find that at all difficult?

Fox: No, sir.

But the lies, what about them? What about claiming to be a farmer, a man of independent means, 'something in the insurance line'? What about the flour mill-owning father? And saying he went to Framlingham College? Why did he tell such lies?

Fox: To impress people.

So Cassels presented the jury with a romancer and fraudster, but nothing more. A murderer? Surely not! And surely not the murderer of his own mother – it was too horrible to contemplate. Finally, Cassels emphasised that all the young man was doing was to improve his mother's life. Where was the crime in that?

In response, the prosecution called 72 witnesses. Samuel Hopkins, who had dragged Rosaline out of the smoke-filled room gave evidence:

Attorney General: What part did Fox play while you were doing all this?

Witness: None whatsoever, sir.

It was the kind of answer that worries jurors. They do not like men who stand back when their mothers, their wives, their lovers are in danger of

Sir.

The point has been very much stressed at this trial regarding my mother's physical disabilities. I think it should be made plain that although she certainly did suffer from attacks of giddiness & fainting & did walk with a shuffle, she was in other ways quite in normal health for her age.

It is strongly suggested that on account of her weakness she could not if attacked have put up any resistance. It would be wrong to say this, & I think in view of the fact that so recent as May 6 months before death she was examined by a Norwich doctor who certified she was in a normal state of health for her years. Then considering the fact that as recent as 3 weeks before her death she travelled over a good portion of Belgium & France, went all over the Battlefields, had to walk of course.

I am afraid the Jury may think that in the words of the Attorney General "this poor old woman infirm, lying in bed if attacked would not be able to put up any fight at all.

Please forgive me for offering this information.

A letter written by Fox denying his mother was as physically feeble as had been made out in court.

losing their lives. Why had Sidney done nothing more to help than raise the alarm?

On the seventh day of the trial, Sidney was questioned for five hours. The most telling exchange occurred when he was asked why he had not left open the door of his mother's room when he saw the smoke.

Fox: I don't remember what I did but my explanation now is that it was so that the smoke should not get about in the hotel.

Attorney General: Rather that your mother should suffocate in that room than the smoke should get about in the hotel?

No matter how he wriggled, claiming to forget what he had done, suggesting he had acted in panic, Sidney's credibility suffered a huge dent in this particular exchange. The jury saw through him.

The Attorney General saw through Sidney, too, describing him as 'a young man of intelligence and a considerable degree of self-possession.' In passing sentence, Mr Justice Rowlett observed that Sidney had been able to get away with what he did until now because he had a 'magnificent way of talking'.

But how long could he have sustained such a life, no matter how persuasive his tongue? Fox must have realised that time was running out and his mother's death was the only solution to his problems. It all seems so short-sighted and short-term – and indescribably callous.

Sidney Fox was executed on 8 April 1930, the last man to be hanged at Maidstone.

9

A VERY
SAD LIFE

The murders of Dorothy and Freda Fisher, and Charlotte
Saunders at Matfield,
July 1940

It was early evening when the police
arrived at Crittenden Cottage on the outskirts of the exquisitely
beautiful Matfield. In a ditch in the orchard, about 40 yards apart, lay
Dorothy Fisher and her 19 year old daughter, Freda. On a path outside
the house Charlotte Saunders, their housekeeper, sprawled. All had
been shot.

The door of the handsome cottage had been left open. Inside, the
writing desk drawers were pulled out. On the kitchen floor was a tea
tray and shattered crockery. Scattered about the floors of the upstairs
bedrooms were the contents of the chests of drawers.

Breaking and entering? A burglary gone wrong? The police were not
convinced. Money in the house had not been taken; jewellery was left
untouched; in Mrs Fisher's handbag there was 14s 3d. What sort of
burglar could this be?

And the broken crockery? There were only three women in the
house yet there were cups, saucers and plates for four. Had someone
been expected? A friend?

And what was the significance of the glove found in the orchard? And
what about the abandoned bicycle discovered by the roadside not far
from Crittenden Cottage?

The Fishers were not well known in the village. Until recently they
had used the cottage only at weekends, but they had moved in
permanently to escape the bombing in London.

Crittenden Cottage at Matfield, where three women died in 1940. (Photo – Sue Edwards)

Walter Fisher visited his wife and daughter quite regularly. Although separated they were on excellent terms. He had taken a farm in Oxfordshire where he lived with an exotic widow, Florence Iris Ouida Ransom, who in spite of a choice of three first names was always known as Julie.

It was enough to make tongues wag in that conventional rural world of Kent in 1940, especially when the auburn-haired Julie, expensively dressed, her nails scarlet, came down with Walter to visit Dorothy Fisher. But, of course, Dorothy had had her own particular friend, the Dane, Mr Westergaard, for many years. They were all on good terms. It was all highly civilised in a 'Noel Cowardish' sort of way. Divorce was never discussed.

They had all been together only a week before when Walter and Julie had accompanied Dorothy and Westergaard to Tonbridge police station. They were seeking permission for Westergaard to live at Crittenden Cottage. Regulations did not permit an alien to live in such a sensitive war zone. Despite the fact that Britain was fighting to free Denmark from German occupation, the police declined to grant the Dane's request. Nevertheless this occasion suggests the understanding relationship which existed between the two couples.

On the evening of the murder, London police visited Westergaard in his elegant West End flat. He could shed no light on the affair and his movements on that day, 9th July, could be accounted for. Whoever had pulled the trigger, it was not the Dane.

Detective Chief Inspector Beveridge of Scotland Yard's Murder Squad surveyed the murder scene, interviewed Walter Fisher, but made no immediate headway. But his visit to Carramore Farm near Bicester was interesting. Here he met Julie, believed locally to be Walter's wife. As Walter Fisher was editor of *Automobile Engineering* and obliged to go to his London office each day, Julie looked after the farm. She was assisted by the Guilfords – mother, son Frederick and daughter-in-law Jessie. They had come from London with Julie and seemed to be very old friends. Beveridge was to ponder over the links of all these people with the murders a hundred miles away.

Within days witnesses came forward. A boy had seen a woman looking through the hedge into the orchard of Crittenden Cottage on the day of the murder. A taxi driver and a ticket operator at Tonbridge station recalled a red-headed woman getting off the train at midday. She had been carrying a long, narrow parcel. They also remembered her catching the 4.25 pm train back to London. At Bicester, the Station Master had seen a woman with distinctive red hair joining the 8.56 am London train, as did a ticket collector. William Playfoot, a baker, had given a lift to a woman who was going to Tonbridge from Matfield that afternoon. She had told him a long story about her children being evacuated to Cornwall; about her husband in the RAF; about her mother's illness.

On 12th July the police went back to the farm in Oxfordshire where Frederick Guilford handed over a rifle. Later in the day, Julie was arrested in London by Detective Chief Inspector Beveridge and Superintendent Cook of Tonbridge. Asked to try on the glove found in the orchard, she at first denied it was hers, later remembering that she had given some odd items to Freda. She must have given the girl her gloves, she said. But its mate was never found at the cottage.

At an identity parade at Tonbridge police station the following day, standing in a line-up of women all wearing blue serge trousers, high-heeled shoes and short jackets, Julie was picked out by several witnesses. During a search of the farm, identical items of clothing were found.

When charged with murder she shouted out, 'I didn't do it. How could I?' Later she was to tell the police, 'Not that there is anything to hide but I have had a very sad life and wish it not to be known. I wish to forget it.'

The mysteries of Julie's very sad life were to come out at her trial at the Old Bailey in November 1940.

It transpired that a couple of weeks before the murder, Julie had asked Fred Guilford to teach her to ride a bicycle. He did try, though she was never very proficient. She also asked him if he would teach her to use his shotgun. Again Fred helped though he must have been surprised when she insisted that he did not tell Walter Fisher. She said that Walter did not like her using firearms.

On 9th July, after Walter had left for London at eight o'clock, Julie asked Fred to give a note to his mother. It read:

'Will you come down and see to Mr Fisher and the farm and don't let anybody know I am out? Get Mr Fisher cold dinner and salad and have some yourself. I will try and be back before Mr Fisher arrives. If not I shall be back soon after. Burn this.'

Burn this?

Julie then told Fred that she was ill and intended to spend the rest of the day in bed. No one saw her again at the farm until late evening.

On his return at about seven o'clock, Walter was surprised to find Julie missing. She was usually waiting for him. Upstairs, next to one of the beds, he found a tin containing cartridges for a shotgun. A ramrod was sticking out of a carrier bag. He was nonplussed.

At 8.50 pm Julie came in. She had been in the house all day until late afternoon, she said, and then gone out, looking for a missing cat. In the fields she had fallen down and badly bruised herself. As she felt ill she had called in at Jessie's and had fallen asleep on the bed for several hours.

The truth was that she had taken the train from Bicester to London, where she caught a connection to Tonbridge. Whether or not she took a taxi to Matfield is unclear. The police assumed that she had telephoned the Fishers from Tonbridge to tell them she was coming. Miss Saunders, the housekeeper, a peripheral figure whose ill-luck it was to be in the house that afternoon, had prepared tea.

Once at the cottage, Julie had taken out the shotgun from her long, narrow parcel. Did she say as she loaded it that she was going to pot a

Dorothy Fisher and her daughter Freda in the early 1930s.

rabbit? She had fired and reloaded six times. The reconstruction suggested that she first shot Freda in the back. Then she chased Dorothy, shooting her in the head and as her quarry lay there, she had shot her once more in the back. Somewhere, dashing around in the orchard, Julie dropped her glove. Miss Saunders, preparing tea in the kitchen and seeing what was happening, dropped the tray. Leaving the house, she was intercepted and shot in the head. Two more rounds were pumped into Freda's back as she lay on the ground.

There was a cycle at the cottage which Julie now took. Sadly, her lessons with Fred Guilford availed little. Only a few yards up the road she fell off, leaving the cycle, its handlebars twisted, by a gate. It must have been a heavy fall for her thigh and knee were badly bruised. Later that day she was to invent the story of having fallen down in the field to explain these bruises.

It cannot be said at what time Julie returned to the farm. She caught the 4.25 pm train from Tonbridge to London and ought therefore to have been home before Walter. Most likely she returned home later, calling in on Jessie Guilford for a few minutes before going up to the house.

On 10th July, Mrs Guilford had asked Julie where she had been the day before. The old lady clearly had doubts about her. Julie said that she had been out in his car with Dudley Benjafield, a doctor. Why then, Mrs Guilford asked, had she told Walter a different story? 'I can't tell Mr Fisher,' Julie answered. 'He wouldn't understand that kind of relationship.' Again she begged Mrs Guilford not to say she had been absent all day. But surely now Mrs Guilford had some idea of where Julie had really been?

Jessie too must have wondered. Julie had not been on her bed for several hours the previous evening as she had told Walter Fisher. She had been only minutes at her cottage.

As for Fred, he had asked where his shotgun and cartridges were. There was a licence problem, Julie told him. She would attend to it. And the cartridges? They had got damp, she told Fred, and she had thrown them away.

Why on earth did these three people accept these absurd stories? That they must very quickly have realised Julie's involvement in a most horrific slaughter cannot be doubted. And even Walter Fisher must have feared the truth of the matter.

So why did none of them challenge her? Perhaps Walter did not because he was having difficulties in bringing himself to accept the possibility of his lover having committed such an atrocity. But the problem the others experienced was more complex. For the Guilfords were not simply old friends of Julie. Mrs Guilford was her mother. Fred was her brother and Jessie her sister-in-law. And incredibly, Walter Fisher was unaware of this relationship until the police enquiries exposed it.

Why this fiction was maintained over at least five years – the length of time Julie had known Walter Fisher – has not been satisfactorily explained. Was Julie ashamed of her modest connections, yet rather than cut her family out of her life, did she allow them into it on conditions? Or was it an expression of Julie's eccentricity? But why did the other three collude in such a bizarre fiction?

The prosecutor at Julie's trial, Mr St John Hutchinson, said: 'It was a very carefully planned out murder.' Not only had she arranged an alibi for herself at the farm but at the cottage, after the shooting, she had remembered to pick up the cartridge cases.

In court, evidence of what Julie had called her 'very sad life' was brought up. She had a long history of mental instability. Even the prosecution counsel accepted that she was 'a highly hysterical woman'. She had suffered from convulsions, memory loss, giddiness and most recently at the farm 'a brainstorm or a collapse'. Letters read in court which she had recently written to Dorothy Fisher, who regarded her as a friend, betrayed an unstable character.

The reason for the dreadful slaughter at Crittenden Cottage can only be that Julie was brooding on her uncertain position. She was not married to Walter: he and his wife had never considered divorce. What if they decided to come together again, she must have asked herself. Was it a mixture of anxiety and jealousy which drove her over the edge? If so, it was not necessary. Walter had taken out a huge insurance policy in her favour. She was assured of the farm if he should die and she could have gone on living there for the rest of her days.

Uncertainty and jealousy. Perhaps these nagged away at her. Perhaps she saw only one way out.

Florence Iris Ouida Ransom was found guilty of triple murder. The death sentence was commuted and she spent the rest of her days in Broadmoor.

10

DEATH AT
THE PLAZA

The murder of George Roberts at Dover,
July 1941

The Temples of Dreams, that's what
they were called, all those Odeons, Ritzes, Regals, Palladiums, Queens.
Such grand places, luxurious, where you could be whisked away to
realms of fancy, worlds of magic.

At least that was how it was for the audience. Until Saturday they
were showing *Arise My Love* at the Plaza. Next week it was to be
Hurricane and *The Prisoner of Zenda*. Wonderful escapes. But as far as
Sidney Williams was concerned there was nothing particularly
glamorous about the Plaza in the Metropole Buildings at Dover. He
started work after the last performance ended at 9.30 pm, staying all
night as cleaner and nightwatchman, on the look-out in case Jerry
dropped incendiaries on the building. To him the night of 3rd July 1941
seemed much like any other as he set about cleaning the empty
auditorium.

It was a lonely job but at least in a way George Roberts was company
for the cleaner. Though they did not meet that night, Williams assumed
that the manager was in his office as usual. Sleeping there. Ever since
his transfer from the ABC cinema at Chatham, Mr Roberts had rolled out
his mattress in his office, taken his pillow out of the cupboard and spent
the night there. Well, digs were costly and his home was in Gillingham.
It did not seem a bad arrangement.

Williams worked through until eight o'clock the next morning. Then
the women cleaners came in. They were responsible for the offices and
staff rooms and the vestibule.

When Mrs Foot went to the female staff room she noticed that the

The programme at the Plaza when George Roberts met his death in 1941.

photo frame and the vase which were usually on the window sill had been transferred to a shelf. And on the tiled floor she saw a dark stain which she scrubbed off.

Mrs Southwell saw a stain, too, on the manager's carpet, and assuming that he had been sick, tackled the mark with disinfectant. A couple of towels were also missing. The mattress was rolled up as usual but unusually, on top of it, were Mr Roberts' pyjamas and dressing gown. She was used to seeing the mattress, the pillow even, but it was the first time she had seen the manager's nightwear.

When Mrs Roberts – no relation of the manager – started to dust the office she noticed the bunch of keys on the desk. They belonged to Mr Roberts, she knew that. But he'd never left them out before.

Though all three cleaners noticed something slightly odd, they did not think of mentioning these matters to each other. After all, cleaners take it all in their stride – stains, spills, furniture changes, minor carelessnesses.

It was only later when Mr Roberts' secretary, Ellen Tolputt, arrived at 10.30 am that anyone expressed surprise at the manager's absence. Finding the keys on the desk, Miss Tolputt opened the safe. Where was the £3 float? Wasn't one of the blue canvas bags missing?

Uneasy, Miss Tolputt telephoned the Granada ABC Cinema, whose manager, Sidney Sale, was senior to Mr Roberts. In response to her call, one of the assistant managers came round to the Plaza. Together, he and Miss Tolputt counted the cash still in the safe. They expected a sum in excess of £40 but over £32 was missing.

Cash missing? A manager missing? They sent for Mr Sale. And Mr Sale, who had had until now a high regard for the 50 year old George Roberts, put two and two together. Concluding that he had gone off with the cash, he called in the police.

Detective Inspector Datlen and Detective Constable Thain of the local CID came to the cinema. Miss Tolputt explained to them that she had seen Roberts at 10.30 the night before, as he was returning to the Plaza after a brief visit to the nearby Friends Social Club. The detectives inspected the marks on the carpet. In the female staff room their attention was drawn to the window ledge. Peering down from the window to the cemented basement area they could make out a reddish mark that looked as if it had been brushed.

The detectives, accompanied by Sale, decided to look inside the disused basement. With torches they inspected a workshop and some small rooms. Sale went into one of them: 'I went into the recess at the far end of the room and there I found Mr Roberts.'

The top of the dead man's head was split open. On the right side, there were three wounds, two of which had deeply penetrated the skull. Two other heavy blows had been delivered to the back of the head.

Immediately Scotland Yard was informed and two specialist officers, Superintendent William Rawlings and Detective Sergeant Marshall, were sent to Dover to work with Inspector Datlen.

From the start the police were confident that whoever had committed the brutal murder knew about the manager's habits and the cinema's interior. There were no signs of a break-in and no fingerprints of any help to the investigators. The staff were interviewed and asked to make statements. Some items of their clothing were sent off to the Hendon Police Laboratory, as was the heavily bloodstained axe which had been found in the basement rooms. On the face of it, however, all staff had sound alibis.

Despite energetic enquiries and scores of interviews, no arrest was made. The last two murders in Dover had occurred in 1936 and they had been speedily resolved. This time, however, in its 18th July 1941 edition, the *Dover Express* opined that 'it appears as though this, Dover's first mystery murder, will be an unsolved one, unless someone who could speak does not persist in remaining silent.'

And the motive, locals asked, what could it be? Was it simply robbery? Or revenge? Had Roberts a secret enemy?

Then, quite out of the blue, on 21st July an arrest was made. On the afternoon of that day Superintendent Rawlings asked 18 year old Leslie Hammond to come to the police station. Hammond, one of the four operators at the Plaza, had already made a written statement and Rawlings had been reconsidering it. There was a matter he wished to clear up.

Hammond had stated that he had been outside the Plaza talking to his brother until 9.55 pm. He was due to do fire-watching duty later and having time to fill in, he had gone for a stroll. He described a roundabout route he had followed taking in Cannon Street, the Market Square, the Monument, Northampton Street and several others until he turned back into the High Street. He had eventually reached the Midland Bank where he was to fire-watch at eleven o'clock. The walk had taken him 65 minutes.

Rawlings had followed the same route. It had taken him 44 minutes. Could Hammond account for the 21 minute discrepancy, the detective asked. And supplementary to that, why had Hammond given the wrong time for his arrival at the Midland Bank? He had not turned up until 11.30 pm. Now the discrepancy was 51 minutes. Did he have an explanation?

Hammond hesitated for five minutes before attempting to answer the Superintendent's question. Finally he spoke: 'I cannot think. When they talk about Mr Roberts I get a funny feeling here [pointing to his head]. I feel I went back to the Plaza but I can't think.'

Superintendent Rawlings told the boy to take his time, to try to remember what happened on the night of the manager's murder. Eventually, Hammond was persuaded to pick up a pen. He now wrote a new statement for the detectives, confessing to the murder.

Hammond had gone back into the cinema sometime after ten o'clock and had waited in a side vestibule for Roberts to come in from the Friends Social Club. When he saw the manager arriving he had darted into the switch room for the axe he had taken from the re-wind room earlier in the day.

'I then went out into the vestibule,' Hammond told the police, 'and hit Mr Roberts with the axe. He fell down and I struck him in the face. Then his head was bleeding so I tied a tablecloth round it and then carried him into the female staff room.'

Hammond had planned to hide the body in the little-used basement but could not take it through the auditorium or other public areas as the night cleaner might see him. Instead, he threw the corpse out of the female staff room window into the basement area, a drop of over twelve feet.

'I went through the hall, through the front vestibule, through the communicating door, down the steps into the basement. Then I dragged him to the entrance to the large workshop. Then through the workshop and into the second little room.'

Hammond returned to the office and wiped the floor with towels taken out of the cupboard. He took Roberts' overcoat and put it over the body. Then he washed away the blood in the entrance.

The statement continues: 'I went into the office again and saw the keys of the safe on the floor. I opened the safe and took out some money. I locked the safe and put the keys on the desk. I picked up the axe and went into the female staff room, got on to the table and threw the axe through the window into one of the rooms in the basement below the window ... I went to the gents and was sick.'

Hammond left the building unnoticed by the night cleaner and went the short distance to the Midland Bank for his fire-watching duties, arriving at 11.30 pm. His activity in the Plaza, murdering Roberts, disposing of the corpse, clearing up, had taken over an hour.

After some days he must have begun to feel secure. The police seemed to have come to a halt in their investigations. And then suddenly Superintendent Rawlings had called him in and his whole story crumbled.

Everything came out. Some of the money he had hidden in a cistern in a public lavatory. In the outside lavatory at his house there was a parcel tied with tape. In it were notes to the value of £18, a tidy sum of money for someone on a weekly wage of £1 12s 6d. When he was strip-searched, a crumpled bag for silver coins was found hidden in his underpants, though why he had kept it there is unclear. The bag was clearly marked 'Plaza Cinema, Dover'. It was also initialled 'RW' in pencil: Rose Williams was the cinema's cashier.

'I don't know why I done it,' Hammond told the police.

Charged with murder in September 1941, Hammond was tried over two days at the Old Bailey. The case against him seemed watertight. However, early in the proceedings his counsel, Mr Waddy, had a submission to make and the judge, in accordance with counsel's wishes, asked the jury to withdraw.

Hammond's statement, Waddy claimed, was not admissible. It was damning to any defence and if the prosecution were to open the case with it, Hammond would have no chance. Waddy's claim was that Hammond had been ill-treated by the police, making his statement on 21st July 1941 under duress. Waddy was then allowed to question the three police officers who had conducted the interview.

The judge, Mr Justice Cassels, then heard lengthy legal argument and evidence about the admissibility of Hammond's statement. In the end, however, he rejected the defence's case. He regarded what Hammond had said as voluntary.

The jury returned to the courtroom. The prosecution read out the statement that Hammond had made and all was now lost. Suggestions of insanity were rejected and, inevitably, Hammond was found guilty. He was sentenced to death.

In October 1941 Hammond appealed against his conviction, the hearing taking place before the Lord Chief Justice and Justices Humphreys and Lewis. The matter turned once more on the admissibility of his statement. The appeal was rejected.

'We cannot entertain the smallest doubt,' said Mr Justice Humphreys, 'that the accused was rightly convicted on evidence which was properly before the jury and we are satisfied that the confession was rightly admitted in evidence.'

Nevertheless, on 11th November 1941, on the eve of what would have been his execution, the Home Secretary granted a reprieve and Hammond was sentenced to life imprisonment.

Hammond's was a drab little crime. It lacked the drama that an audience at the Plaza might have looked for. No thrills, no glamour, just a squalid affair. Not fitting, they might have said, for a Temple of Dreams.

11

MORE OR LESS
ON THE RAMPAGE

The death of Anthony Crean at Shorne,
March 1975

You will certainly find Shorne on the map. On most maps anyway. There it is between Gravesend and Rochester, somehow tucked away, still resolutely rural yet only a short distance from motorways, industry, high-rises, crowds. Search the guide books, look in the glossy 'Garden of England' coffee-table books, hunt out the serious histories of the county, and you will be unlikely to find much mention of Shorne. Perhaps it is too small, perhaps not enough happens there. Truth is, it is a sleepy little village, though none the worse for that.

It suited Anthony Crean. He liked it well enough. He had been settled there for three years and it was just his sort of place, where he could take long walks with his Jack Russell terrier, where he could have leisurely chats with the people he had come to live among. He liked them, that was evident, and they liked him. He was always in and out of Corpus Christi convent, going there every evening for supper at 6.30 from his house next door. Father Anthony Crean, now 63 and in semi-retirement, acted as chaplain to the little religious community.

So when on 21st March 1975, a Friday, Father Crean was found dead in the bath of his home, fully clothed, stabbed about the body and with his skull gaping open with deep wounds, the village was horrified. How could anyone have done such a fearful, brutal thing? And of all people, to the priest?

It was the nuns who had first alerted the police. Father Crean, most unlike him, had not turned up for his supper. Strange that he had not mentioned that he would not be coming. After all, St Katherine's

Patrick Mackay in London. (Piers Morgan, *Chatham, Rochester & Gillingham News*)

Cottage where he lived was just yards away from the convent. Not that the nuns had been unduly anxious. Not until someone came to the door with the Jack Russell. It had been found straying in the village: its finder had taken it to the priest's house but there had been no reply.

When they entered the house, now fearful that something was wrong, the sisters found the body in the bathroom.

It was well on in the evening when the police arrived. Detective Chief Inspector Lew Hart, head of Medway CID, initiated a painstaking hunt of the locality, searching for the murder weapon. Tracker dogs were brought in to comb the area. Eventually, in a cupboard at St Katherine's Cottage a heavily blood stained axe was found.

Fortunately the brain, its memory, and its instincts come into play, very often bypassing the need for other recording systems. At Shorne, Detective Inspector Ken Tappenden recalled that a couple of years earlier Father Crean had had his cheque book stolen. A Gravesend man, Patrick Mackay, had been apprehended, though not before he had helped himself to £80. The police had proceeded with charges although the priest, who had earlier befriended the young man, had tried to persuade them not to do so. In the event, Mackay had been charged with breaking and entering, fined £20, and ordered to repay the money at £7 a month. In nearly two years, nothing had been repaid. Could the same man be responsible for this horrifying murder? Had he come back to the victim of his earlier offence? Criminals often do return to victims and crime scenes to repeat their offences or to commit new ones. At least, in Tappenden's view, it was worth looking Mackay up.

Whilst other leads were being followed, Detective Sergeant Bob Brown and Detective Constable Michael Whitlock were sent to London in the early hours of the Saturday morning. At Scotland Yard they checked on Mackay's record and found that the 23 year old former Gravesend school caretaker, gardener and odd-job man had been convicted eleven times on charges of robbery, theft and violence. Then, equipped with a couple of dozen addresses at any of which the man they sought might be found, Brown and Whitlock began a dogged and demanding non-stop search for their man.

In Mackay's bedsit at a probation hostel in Great North Road, Finchley, the detectives found a quantity of stolen jewellery. They also found a mass of Nazi propaganda. Pictures of Adolf Hitler adorned the walls of the room.

The two policemen must have wondered what in Nazism could appeal to a man like Patrick Mackay. Not the political theory, surely;

not spurious notions of socialism. More likely, from his record, it would lie in the obscene brutalities which disfigured the Third Reich. His admiration would be directed towards the chaos, the notion of barbaric misrule which underlay that regime. The worst images of Nazism, the coarse visions, were what this man would admire.

Brown and Whitlock had perhaps little time throughout that long Saturday to reflect on the distortions of politics. Throughout the day their laborious trawl from address to address met with false information, hints, suggestions, some positive help, some stonewall denials. At last, however, their solid old-fashioned policing paid off. Early on the Sunday morning they unearthed their quarry in a house in Stockwell. A hefty six footer, he surrendered to them without resistance.

At Clapham police station, Patrick Mackay admitted to Father Crean's murder. He made the following statement to Chief Inspector Hart:

'I went to Gravesend last Friday afternoon, 21st March 1975. I won a chicken in a raffle like I told you and took it home for my mother to cook for me. I talked with my mother but I was only at home for about 15 minutes. I'm not at all sure about the times but I left the house about half past four. I walked to Father Crean's house at Shorne. From my own house I went along Thong Lane to a country lane that branches off from Thong Lane. I walked all along that lane past the school at Shorne, through Shorne village, past the Rose and Crown, turned left and down the hill to Father Crean's house.

'When I got there I saw the front door was slightly ajar, just enough to put a finger in. I saw his car there and I saw smoke from a bonfire at the back of the house so I knew Father Crean was in. I pushed the door open and a little dog brushed past my legs and ran out of the door. It was Father Crean's dog. I had seen it when I have been there before. I don't know where the dog went but I think it might have run out of the gate. I went into the hall of the house and called, "Mr Crean. Are you there?" I wanted to talk with him over this money because things were unsettled the last time I saw him. There was no reply so I knocked on the door to the left. It was locked. From there I walked to the back of the hall where there was a bike. I stood around waiting for him. From there I decided to go into the kitchen. I looked through his bedroom door to see if he was in and if he might not have been asleep – that is the bedroom on the ground floor. As he wasn't there I went upstairs and had a look around up there. Then I came back downstairs and waited in his bedroom doorway for his return. After about five minutes, that is from the time I first went into the house, I heard the front door open and then saw Mr Crean come into the hall. He didn't seem to see me. He unlocked the door to his front room. He seemed to be standing in the doorway, doing something to his pipe, I think lighting it.

'I walked up to him and when I was about an arm's length away I said, "Mr Crean, it's me, Patrick Mackay." He had his back to me. He turned round and he shouted, "Oh God, I wasn't expecting to see you here." I said, "I've come to talk things over about the money I owe you." He seemed to panic a bit and started to run out of the house. This seemed to upset me a bit as I had basically come to explain things to him about this money. I grabbed hold of him by his arm, I think the right one, and we both fell on the floor in the hallway. I struggled and he struggled on the floor and he seemed to get extremely nervy. He said, "Don't hurt me." This seemed to get me even more excitable myself and then I started to strike him on the side of the head with my hand and with my fist. The next thing I knew he had broken loose from my grip and ran into the bathroom which is just off the hallway.

'Whilst I had been on the floor of the hallway myself I picked up an axe from a box lying just under the stairs and I began to feel even more excitable. I pulled out a knife from my pocket – no, that is wrong – that was later. He shut the bathroom door and pushed to hold it closed. I barged my side of the door and this pushed him towards the bath. He tumbled and half fell into the bath. I threw down the axe on to the floor and pushed him into the bath. He then started to annoy me even more and I kept striking at his nose with my arm and the side of my hand. I then pulled out my knife from my coat pocket and repeatedly plunged it into his neck. I then got a little more excitable and stuck it into the side of his head and then tried to plunge it into the top of his head. This bent the knife. I grabbed for the axe and with this repeatedly lashed out with it at his head. He sank into the bath. He had been in the sitting-up position with the knife, but when I first hit him with the axe he sank down into the bath. I then repeatedly got increasingly more annoyed and lashed at him with the axe.

'All this seemed to happen very fast. I threw the axe to the floor, ripped the plug from the wash-basin and rammed it into the bath, then turned on the taps. I had mainly the cold water tap on but I'm not sure whether I turned them off or left them at the time I left. I believe I may have turned them off. I then turned on the bathroom light, his bedroom light and his hall light. Then I stayed in the bathroom for about an hour. I was just watching him sinking and floating about in the bath and then

I walked out of the house and walked around to the back of the house picking up bits and pieces of cinders from the fire, just mucking about, doodling in a sense. Then I went back in the house and into the bathroom and stayed there for about a quarter of an hour.

'I then thought of the chicken at my mother's house and walked out of his house altogether. I passed his car on the way out and walked to the right of the gate. This took me on to a narrow country lane which I walked up. I turned to my right and this took me back to the lane I originally used to travel down to his home. I walked along there and this took me about an hour. My throat seemed very dry and I saw a cottage. I went through a gate, knocked on the door and asked a man for a drink of water. He gave me one. I thanked him and walked home for the chicken at my mother's house. I talked to her and she gave me the chicken and I ate most of it there.

'I caught a bus into town, went to the pictures like I told you and caught a train to Waterloo. I threw the knife into the Thames from Hungerford Bridge on realizing I had it in my pocket. I had thrown the axe into the tool-box in the hall after I left the bathroom. The other knife I told Mr Brown about today I kept. I'm not sure whether I used this knife at the house or whether I kept it in my pocket. The only thing I want to add is it didn't seem to trouble me too much what I had done on hearing it was in the papers.'

There were further revelations. At first these were less horrifying than what Mackay had already confessed. 'I have bag snatched and bashed a lot of old ladies,' he told the arresting officers. Over the months he had terrorised Knightsbridge in an orgy of muggings and robberies. In court he was to ask for 24 such offences to be taken into consideration.

And there were other offences, too. During the time awaiting trial, Mackay confided in his fellow prisoners. Father Crean was not his only murder victim. He had committed other murders, he told his listeners. He had murdered eleven people. The police were informed. This was no ordinary cell-mate after all.

So now Mackay was being questioned about Miss Mary Hynes, a crippled 73 year old found battered to death with her stockings pushed down her throat at her home in Kentish Town in July 1973.

There were questions, too, about a death in the following February, when a surgeon's widow, 84 year old Isabella Griffiths, was discovered stabbed to death in the locked kitchen of her home in fashionable Cheyne Walk, Chelsea. Admitting this murder, Mackay recalled that he had stabbed the old woman so fiercely that her body had been pinned to the floor. But this was not true, the police pointed out. Another female, however, had been found elsewhere, the knife through her body embedded in the floorboards. But for this murder Mackay stoutly denied responsibility.

In June 1974, a 63 year old tobacconist, Leslie Goodman, had been bludgeoned to death in his Finsbury Park shop. Police questioned Mackay about this murder.

More recently, on 10th March, only two weeks before the murder at Shorne, the 89 year old widow of a big game hunter, Adele Price, had been strangled in her Lowndes Square flat in Belgravia. Mackay was questioned about this and several other horrific murders – a German au pair thrown off a train at London Bridge; a widow and her 4 year old grandson; a down-and-out thrown over Hungerford Bridge; a lady who owned a cafe at Southend, axed to death. Mackay denied these killings and only the Belgravia case was brought to court. For this murder he was found guilty. Police believed him to be responsible for some of the other killings though no charges were made.

Mackay's past history was a catalogue of crime leading almost inexorably to an unbridled two-year climax of terror. His father had shown the way with his violence towards his wife and children before dying, a chronic alcoholic, at the age of 52. At school in Gravesend, young Patrick was a bully and a torturer of pet animals. In his early teens he had been on probation and twice in the course of two years had been sent to approved school. At this time, a Home Office psychiatrist had described the 15 year old as 'a cold, psychopathic killer'. From then the nature of his criminality became increasingly apparent. In 1968, when only 16, he had attempted to strangle his mother. There followed a brief stay in a mental hospital. On his release he assaulted other members of his family. In the same year, Mackay was arrested for robbery and returned to the mental hospital for 14 months. Then, at home once more, he terrorised his mother and sisters, on one occasion barricading himself in his room and threatening suicide.

There followed three years in mental wards where he committed violent assaults on nurses and other patients. Discharged in 1972, he was re-admitted the following year as a voluntary patient. Early in 1974, after again making threats to kill himself, he was placed in Tooting Bec Mental Hospital but absconded from there. And now the murders began.

Mackay had known Mrs Griffiths, although how far back this

Patrick Mackay, serial killer. (Piers Morgan, *Chatham Rochester & Gillingham News*)

association went is unclear. It might have been no more than a matter of weeks. He had once kindly offered to carry her shopping bag and she had asked him back to run errands and do odd jobs for her. A neighbour told the police, 'I think the man who killed her used to help her in the house from time to time. He seemed a nice young man.'

Certainly, he must have appeared trustworthy and responsible for Mrs Griffiths, living on her own, was a nervous woman. But on 14th February 1974, she had no hesitation in taking off the safety chain and admitting the 'nice young man' to her flat. She was throttled, thrown to the ground, and stabbed. Mackay admitted that after this hideous murder he had once more contemplated suicide.

On 10th March 1975, during the time when he was, in his own words, 'more or less on the rampage', Mackay went to Harrods to look for a likely pick-up, anybody who might be 'a fair chance to follow'. But that day there was no potential victim for him. Aimlessly he wandered off to Belgravia and there, in a square, he sat down and drank half a bottle of Scotch.

And then Mrs Price came into view, crossing over to his side of the road. He followed the old woman to Lowndes Square. As she let herself in the main door, Mackay slipped into the lobby with her. He felt faint, he told her. Could he have a drink, he asked, tea or even just a glass of water? And the old lady, anxious to help, let him into her flat. Too late, she realised she had been duped and challenged him.

'She said she thought I must be mad. I told her I didn't want any complications and I was feeling on edge. I said, "This is Belgravia. You must know what I am here for."'

And then, of a sudden, what must have been his plan to rob her changed. 'I told her to go into the bedroom. I went in with her. The next thing I remember I had my hand around her neck.'

It was only days after this that Mackay went to Shorne, back to the home of the priest from whom two years earlier he had stolen a cheque book. What impelled his murderous intent? Did he hold Father Crean responsible for his being caught? Was it some misconceived desire for revenge? Was this some further illogical obsession? Or had he really intended to resolve the matter of his earlier theft, to make arrangements to repay the money? It is not possible to disentangle the truth in the case of a man like Mackay.

At Ashford Remand Centre, after seven months under observation, Patrick Mackay was declared by a consultant psychiatrist to have 'a well masked sadistic interest'. To another leading medical man he was 'a cold psychopathic killer'. What is so unnerving is that in his everyday like Mackay appeared to be normal. He was a classic psychopathic type.

Defending Mackay, who appeared in court charged with five murders, Mr Michael Parker QC recommended a life sentence as much for his client as for the community. He admitted that the present state of medical science held out no immediate hope of treatment for Mackay's condition. At some future time, but only when his condition stabilised, perhaps he might be sent to a secure hospital. Mr Parker expressed the hope that special units for psychopaths might be set up in prisons.

There is some inbuilt confusion in the law – as there has been for the past 150 years – as it relates to criminal insanity and the idea that if a criminal knows his act to be wrong, he must be sane and therefore responsible for his actions. Certainly that was the view expressed by Mr Justice Milmo when passing sentence.

'Medical evidence which has been given by two very eminent psychiatrists', the judge said, 'makes it very clear that you are not insane because you knew what you were doing and you knew that it was wrong. You are a highly dangerous man and it is my duty to protect the public. That I can only do by making an order which will ensure that unless and until you cease to be the menace you now are, you will be kept in secure custody.'

Mackay was sentenced to life imprisonment not for murder but for the manslaughter of three people – two cases were left on file. And at least five other cases were certainly believed by the police to be, if not solved, then no longer requiring further investigation.

12

IN THE
THIRTEEN MINUTE GAP

The murder of Niki Mina at Ashford,
December 1979

When George Mina arrived home
with his six year old son, Niki was not there. Strange. Worrying, really.
It was ten o'clock and his wife ought to have been home by then. She
always caught the bus that left the William Harvey Hospital at Ashford
shortly after nine. It took her straight to the station. It was only a short
train ride from there to Wye. She really ought to be back.

George put young John to bed. They had been up to London for the
day, visiting relatives, and the boy was tired. But this was so unlike
Niki. Perhaps she had missed the train. Or was it late? Perhaps the bus
had left her behind. Impatient and anxious, George got out his cycle
and went out into the chill of the December night. He recalled that Niki
had walked home from the hospital before on a couple of occasions
but that was in the summer. She would not dream of trying to walk
back at such an hour on a winter night. After cycling for hours with no
sign of his wife, George returned home and telephoned the police.

Next day, 17th December 1979, there was still no word. Had she left
him, George wondered, but dismissed the idea. 'We were so very
close,' he told the police later. In any case, she had not taken clothes or
money or her passport. And where would she have gone in England?
They were strangers. They did not even intend to stay once George had
his horticultural degree from Wye College. Then they would be off,
back to the sun and the mountains, back to Cyprus.

'How can you explain it when someone just disappears?' George was
to ask. And Niki was not the sort of woman to go off without warning.
'She was more of an old-fashioned housewife,' he said. She had the

virtues of the mountain village she came from near Limassol. She was reserved, rather shy. And most certainly not the kind of wife to desert her husband and little boy.

The police established that Niki had last been seen coming out of the women's changing room at the hospital at 8.50 pm. Yet she had not boarded the 9.03 pm bus. If something had happened to her, or if she had made a decision to disappear, it had been in that 13 minute gap. The hospital was searched thoroughly but there was no sign of the missing nurse. The tracker dogs found nothing in the grounds nor in the surrounding hedges or ditches.

If the police at first considered this to be a routine missing person enquiry, they recognised three days later that perhaps it was something more serious. At Wrotham, 31 miles away, on the eastbound carriageway of the M20, Niki's handbag and lunch box were found.

Now police mounted a massive search for Niki. Near where her belongings had been found, tons of gravel for motorway works were sifted by men and machines. Four thousand people including 2,000 hospital staff were questioned, some of them on several occasions. Printed notices were distributed describing the missing nurse. She was 5' 1" tall; of Mediterranean appearance with dark brown eyes and chestnut-coloured hair. When last seen she had been wearing a three-quarter length artificial fur coat, slacks and a dark brown woollen hat. She had been carrying the cream leather shoulder bag found at Wrotham.

The police enquiry yielded little at first but they continued their search, constantly questioning, piecing together odd snatches of information. They still believed that the crucial time lay in the 13 minute period. The solution to whatever had happened to Niki Mina would be found in the hospital. The police were convinced of that.

In early February came the breakthrough. Acting on a police request, hospital engineers made an inspection of the underground service tunnels at the hospital. In one of the ducts, 4 feet square and 60 feet long, used in connection with the heating system, the engineers found dried blood, some teeth and hair. At the same time, in the connecting plant room they found two buttons from Niki's coat. Forensic tests proved that the blood, the teeth and the hair also belonged to her. There was no evidence yet, however, that a murder had been committed. Detective Superintendent Earl Spencer made a guarded press announcement: 'We are sure that at the very least she suffered some kind of serious injury and was dragged for some distance along

Excavators on the M20 search for Niki Mina's body. (*The Times*)

the duct, possibly unconscious, and then removed.'

It was clear to the police that only someone with a working knowledge of the hospital would know how to get into the duct, would even know of its existence. And that someone was unlikely to be a doctor or a nurse or a member of the clerical staff. The police were now focusing on people who worked on the maintenance staff, perhaps someone whose duties gave him access to many areas of the hospital, someone who knew the less public parts of the building intimately.

Meanwhile, the distraught George Mina hoped, though not with any degree of optimism, that his wife was still alive.

The persistence of the police and the pressure they were able to exert on a diminished suspect population led finally to an admission of guilt. On 4th March, a young couple were arrested. The next day, police officers were directed to the location of Niki's body. At a hearing before Ashford Magistrates on 6th March, Steven Edwards, a 25 year old former hospital porter, was charged with the murder. His 23 year old wife, Kim, was charged with helping to remove the body and with disposing of evidence. Whilst her husband was on remand, Kim Edwards was bailed to live with her parents.

What subsequently emerged was an horrific tale. It was a murder both astonishing and grisly. But what was it that triggered Steven Edwards to kill Niki Mina? Why did a quiet, responsible young man in the space of so short a time commit this awful crime? Certainly, Edwards' account of what happened is by any standards bizarre.

The trial at Maidstone Crown Court began on 23rd October 1980 and it lasted three and a half days. At the outset defence counsel, Giles Rooke QC, offered a plea of manslaughter which was rejected by the prosecution.

Edwards' statement to the police and the responses he gave in court to questions from both prosecution and defence are the only sources of information for this murder, which had no witnesses.

Edwards described how sometime before nine o'clock on the night of 16th December 1979 he was leaving the plant room at the hospital. As he came out of the door he stepped in front of a nurse who had been walking along the corridor. Perhaps he had come out of the room suddenly, in a rush, say, and had given her a shock. This is what Edwards implied.

'She looked frightened,' he said in his statement, 'and I held up my hand to pacify her.'

We all recognise the sort of incident. It is everyday, commonplace. Someone has a sudden shock as an unexpected figure appears around a corner or from behind a door. In acknowledgement, a hand is raised, palm to the front, making a silent apology. There are smiles. The matter is forgotten. But not this night.

'This only worsened matters,' Edwards went on. 'She started to scream and backed away from me.'

This is undeniably where the doubt creeps in. Did Niki Mina scream straightaway? Had nothing else happened? Or had Edwards by now done something he never admitted? Had Niki Mina realised that something dreadful was about to occur?

'I panicked and thought someone would hear and think I was attacking her. I took hold of her and pulled her back into the doorway of the plant room, hoping to reassure her I had no bad intentions.'

Perhaps that was what some men might do. Unwise, possibly, but not altogether impossible. But in the circumstances, given that she was already screaming and obviously dreadfully frightened, Niki reacted.

'She lashed out at me with her hands and feet. I tried to fight her off and put my hands around her throat.'

If Niki's reaction to meeting Edwards in the corridor seems extreme and irrational, how does his behaviour seem? He had dragged her, a frightened woman, into the plant room doorway and now, as she struggled, he put his hands around her throat.

'Suddenly she sagged at the knees, slipped down the steps and pulled me with her. I landed on top of her. She hit the floor with a terrible thump and appeared to be dead.' And if she was dead, he was saying, it was because he had fallen on top of her.

But now he was desperate, weeping at the predicament in which he found himself. He had been instrumental in killing a girl. It had just happened so quickly. Only seconds ago he had been leaving the plant room: now a girl he did not know lay dead. 'But then I heard a gurgling noise and wondered if it could be her.'

When he looked, there were bubbles of blood coming from her mouth and nose. He thought she must be in great pain although she was still alive. He could have gone for help now but decided not to. There were marks on her throat. He was frightened, in a panic; no one would believe what had occurred. How could they?

'She could have been barely alive. I thought she was going to die so I decided to try and end her pain.'

Ironic, isn't it? Upstairs, men and women spend whole lifetimes saving lives against the odds. Down here, in the plant room, Steven Edwards decides to end a life, thinks about strangling the nurse again. But he cannot. 'I was in a state of exhaustion and could not seem to carry the act out.'

He searched around; found a scaffold pole; returned to her body and struck her twice on the head. They were powerful blows: Niki Mina's injuries were horrific. 'When I struck her,' Edwards said in court, 'I could not tell for sure if she was alive or not.' He took the scaffold pole and washed the blood off it and replaced it where he had found it.

Edwards told the court, 'I did not mean her any harm.' Did this panic-stricken young man really mean that? Had he simply responded blindly in this totally irrational, mad fashion? Was this act totally out of the blue? Or was this his invention, his fiction?

Whatever the truth of it, it was a nightmare which had not finished. Edwards now had to hide the body. Left in the plant room, it would be found the next day.

But the maintenance duct was rarely entered. The body could go in there. And it was quiet now around the hospital. And dark.

So while George Mina cycled the lanes and desperately telephoned the police, Niki lay alone in the duct and Steven Edwards went home to his wife and their two small children. And he could say nothing there about what had happened.

The following day Edwards was on duty on the 2 pm to 10 pm shift.

In the evening, he brought his car round to the rear of the maintenance area. Taking out a plastic mac and a bag, he returned to the duct.

'I was praying the body would not be there and it was all a bad dream,' says the statement. But it was no dream. 'She was in a bit of a mess and I splashed some water about to try and wash the blood away.'

Such understatement this 'bit of a mess'. So as not to leave a trail of blood, he put the bag over the head of the dead woman. And then, sliding the body onto the mac, he dragged it up the slope to his car.

No one saw Steven Edwards in the dark lifting the limp corpse into the boot. That frightful task completed, he returned to his duties, his mind a turmoil, for there was more to be done later.

Just before the end of his shift, Edwards' wife came to the hospital to meet him as she frequently did. It was another dreadful moment in the nightmare which had started 24 hours earlier. Steven Edwards had never had to tell his wife anything as remotely appalling as this: Kim Edwards had no preparation for what she was to hear.

Edwards braced himself. 'I asked her if she loved me and she immediately knew something was wrong.'

How could he bring himself to tell her what had happened? Yet he had to frame the words, make his appalling confession. And when he told her what he had done, when the story came out, she could not believe him. He was joking; he was being silly; such a tale was too outrageous to believe; such horrors did not happen to people like them.

At the last she had no choice but to believe what he said. Instead of rejecting him or denouncing him, Kim was loyal enough to support her husband in what had to be done next.

They drove off, called at Kim's parents and collected their two young children. They were going to visit friends, they said, and wanted the children with them. Now their route took them north, up the M20, through the Dartford Tunnel, along the M25, conscious all the time of the body in the boot and what had to be done with it.

Finally they stopped at what they judged to be a suitable place. They had reached Epping Forest. Edwards lifted the corpse from the boot and carried it over to a tangle of bramble bushes. He placed the body in the middle of these and threw handfuls of leaves over it. With luck it might remain there undetected for years. Kim stayed in the car with the sleeping children whilst her husband completed the task.

On their return journey along the M20, they stopped near Wrotham. Kim took the lunch box, the handbag and Niki's shoes and threw them away. That was her only active part in the whole affair.

In the Crown Court, Mr Rooke, defending Edwards, told the jury that if they believed that Niki died from the blows of the scaffold pole he would concede that this was a case of murder. But he did suggest there must be some doubt. She might have died when Edwards landed on top of her as they fell down the plant room steps. In that case perhaps they ought not to return a verdict of murder.

But the jury was not persuaded by Rooke's interpretation. After an absence of one and a half hours they returned a verdict of guilty. Edwards was sentenced to life imprisonment.

Kim Edwards was found guilty of helping to dispose of the body and some of Niki's belongings. But Mr Justice Milmo was conscious of the fact that she had acted out of a deep sense of loyalty, however mistaken, to her husband. She was sentenced to two years' imprisonment suspended for two years.

Since 17th December when she had first learnt of the murder Kim had hoped that Steven would give himself up. But he had children: he wished to see them grow up. And he still harboured the flickering hope that it would all die down in the end.

But they both knew, of course, that in reality the police would ultimately find them. 'We used our time carefully, knowing we would soon be separated for a very long time,' Kim Edwards said. 'When he eventually did confess I felt a great sense of relief. All that painful waiting was over.'

Steven Edwards went to prison for what does seem to have been an inexplicable, uncharacteristic act of raw violence.

Niki Mina, that temporary visitor to Kent, is buried in her native village. George Mina, the horticulturist, cultivated a new strain of geranium which he named after his wife.

13

THE GARDEN
SHED MURDER

The murder of Gwendoline Marshall at Pluckley,
October 1980

Months later in court, Detective Constable Nicholls described what he saw in the garden shed on the early evening of Wednesday 8th October 1980. Miss Marshall lay on her right side. She was fully dressed, wearing her gumboots. Her face and clothing were soaked in blood. Her left ear was almost severed.

'Her hands had been tied behind her with cord and her head had been struck several times with a blunt instrument,' Nicholls said. 'Her throat had been cut, apparently by a knife. She had been stabbed by a garden or hayfork many times. The hayfork was impaled in her neck.'

The victim had been dead for three or four hours. Some experienced officers thought it one of the most brutal murders they had witnessed.

What could have provoked such an outrage on the body of this old woman, only 4 feet 10 inches tall, not more than seven stone in weight? Those few in Pluckley village who knew Gwendoline Marshall – her gardener, the grocer, the postman – described her as 'the nicest person in the world'. She was a generous, warm-hearted woman, fiercely independent, extremely reserved, and at 79 still looking after herself in the house she had lived in for over 40 years.

In the middle of the afternoon the local constable had received an urgent call to Enfield Lodge, where he met Miss Winter, Gwendoline Marshall's neighbour, and a young couple, the Drylands. When the Drylands had arrived at Miss Marshall's house earlier they had been unable to find her. She had invited them to pick apples in her orchard and they were concerned at her absence. They had asked Miss Winter if she knew what might have happened to her neighbour.

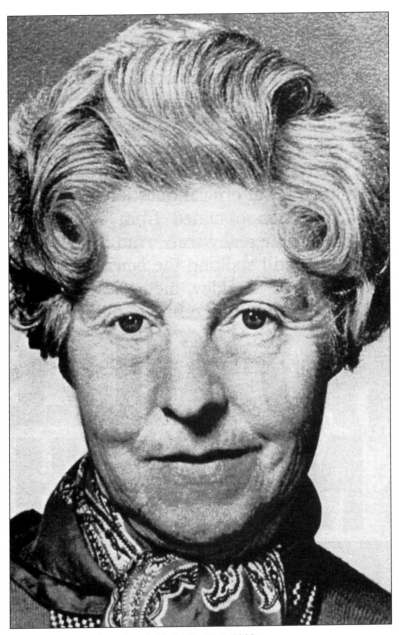

Gwendoline Marshall, murdered at Enfield Lodge in 1980.

Miss Winter had gone to Enfield Lodge with the Drylands. There being no reply to their calls, she and Alan Dryland had entered the house. In the kitchen there was blood on the floor. Had Miss Marshall fallen and hit her head perhaps? But in the lounge the carpet was bloodstained too. On the dining room table a handbag lay open, a chequebook poking out of it. Had someone been rifling it?

Their fears growing, Miss Winter and Dryland searched upstairs. There were smudges, pools, drops of blood in the three bedrooms, the workroom and the bathroom. But of Miss Marshall there was no sign. It was then that they had sent for the local policeman. He recognised immediately that he needed assistance. After all, the house stood in six acres. In the search, the newly arrived officers opened the shed.

By seven o'clock, 70 police officers were making house-to-house enquiries into what was now clearly a case of murder. At eight o'clock, not far from Enfield Lodge, Sergeant Peacock encountered 21 year old Nikki Mannouch from nearby Smarden. The officer recognised the young man who had been before the police on a number of occasions. Where had he been during the day, the sergeant asked. At the Job Centre in Ashford, Mannouch told him. He had caught the 2.23 pm train back to Pluckley. Then he had met Peter Luckhurst.

And Peter Luckhurst, unemployed like his friend Mannouch, was also known to the police, though really he was little more than a nuisance, a petty thief and, in spite of his flaws, a well-liked lad.

Perhaps the police should have a word with Luckhurst, Mannouch suggested. Luckhurst had told him that earlier in the afternoon he had found Miss Marshall's King Charles spaniel, Sophie, in the road outside the house. He had put her over the fence into the garden.

When Sergeant Peacock met Luckhurst on his bicycle shortly afterwards, he questioned him too. No, the youth said, he had not seen Miss Marshall since the day before.

Something ought now to be said about the relationship between Peter Luckhurst, the council house boy, and the wealthy Miss Marshall. The unreliable youngster and curiously reclusive old lady had a warm regard for each other. His mother, who had died five years earlier, had been Miss Marshall's daily help and he knew her well. He visited her quite frequently.

The old spinster was a kind of mother to the boy. Just as Eileen Pollard, his primary school head teacher, seems to have been. Several other people, too, had a soft spot for young Luckhurst. He was undoubtedly something of a rascal but not in any vicious way. In all that has been written and said about Peter Luckhurst, it is evident that many people genuinely liked him.

On the day after the murder, Thursday 9th October, the police picked up Luckhurst and Mannouch and took them to Ashford police station. Perhaps they could help with enquiries they were told, answer a few routine questions.

Mannouch again told the police of his visit to Ashford Job Centre the day before. He had arrived back in Pluckley shortly after 2.30 pm and had gone to Luckhurst's house. The boy seemed not to be himself that afternoon, Mannouch said. 'I have known him a long time and when I was in the house he was very quiet and did not talk much. Normally he is sort of noisy and mucked about a lot.'

Mannouch was questioned very closely about his alibi. If he had travelled on the 2.23 pm from Ashford which reached Pluckley at 2.32 pm, it seemed to rule him out as a suspect for the estimated time of death lay between 1.45 pm and 2.30 pm. It has to be said, of course, that such estimates are not always reliable.

'That old lady', Luckhurst told his interviewers, 'was like a mother to me. I would not even slap her around the face.' When it was suggested that perhaps he and Mannouch had acted in concert and had killed her, he strenuously denied the possibility. 'No way am I going to say my mate killed her ... If I were to say we had done it and my mate had an alibi, then I would get done for twenty years. I may as well just kill myself.'

Experienced interviewers sense the moment to risk the crucial question. If it is posed at the wrong moment, the interviewee will back off, become defensive, will resist. But now seemed the right time to put the question to the 17 year old: 'Peter, what happened when you went into the house yesterday?'

'I didn't go round there yesterday.'

'It has become obvious to me', the officer pressed, 'that you went in there on your own and for some reason something happened, whether you intended it or not.'

There was a pause. 'I hit her with a log,' Luckhurst said after a silence. 'I wanted some money. I had too much to drink.'

He had battered her, half-dragged, half-carried her round the house, looking for money. Then, he told the policemen, he had 'got her to the shed, tied her hands, pushed her to the floor ... I gave her a hefty kick. I don't know why I kicked her.'

Eventually Luckhurst was ready to make his statement which he

The Spectre, where Peter Luckhurst spent the hours before Miss Marshall's murder.

wrote himself. A full-time school truant since the age of twelve, he was still capable of writing a lucid account.

'I had known Miss Marshall for a long time but only through my mother. I left The Spectre Inn at around two o'clock. From there I went into my house, got my bike and went to Enfield Lodge where I left my bike and entered the house. On entering I saw Miss Marshall and I grabbed a log and hit her. I asked have you got any money. She replied no. So I hit her again on the head trying to knock her out but failing this I got angry and forced her around upstairs and downstairs of the house but I could find no money at all except a cheque book which was no use at all so I left it. I hit her again this time knocking out the lady. While unconscious I got her to the shed and tied her hands and pushed her on the floor and kicked her and I went all weird and started hitting her with a fork. On recovering from the funny turn I locked the door and ran like hell. I got on my bike and went home and into my shed. From my shed I saw Nick Mannouch walking past. I asked him where he was going. He said up to the village so I went with him to get his bike which he'd left there and we then went back to my house where I ate my tea and left for Smarden.'

Everything that Peter Luckhurst said seemed to fit the situation and the police were satisfied that they had so quickly caught the murderer.

A kitchen knife with an eight inch blade was found in a drawer in Luckhurst's house. It was subjected to forensic tests as were his clothes and his shoes. The blade of the knife, a small area on the sleeve of his jacket, the bottom of his trousers, his shoes – all were spattered with the blood of the same group as that of the murdered woman. The case against Peter Luckhurst appeared impregnable.

The five-day trial took place at Maidstone Crown Court in June 1981. By now, however, claiming that the police had put him under pressure, Luckhurst had withdrawn his confession.

In court, Luckhurst explained how at about 11.30 am on the day of the murder he had gone to The Spectre, where he had drunk beer and played pool. He had stayed there until about two o'clock when he had gone home for his bicycle. He had decided to go to Enfield Lodge to ask Miss Marshall if she had any work for him. When he received no reply at the house, he had gone inside.

'I saw some blood on the floor. I picked up a log and saw there was some blood on it. I dropped it and went into another room and saw blood marks on the floor. In the kitchen there was blood on the kitchen unit.'

Luckhurst again called out for Miss Marshall but there was still no answer. After looking round the house, he went into the garden and then across to the shed. He described finding the body.

'She was bloody. I knelt down next to her. I prodded her in the back a couple of times to see if she would move. A hayfork was stuck in her neck and I pulled it out. I could not hear her breathing and thought she was dead.'

Then, the young man described how he had replaced the hayfork in the dead woman's neck. After that he ran outside, padlocked the door and went off home on his cycle as fast as he could.

If Peter Luckhurst was hoping that the jury would accept his tale, he did little to endear himself to them. In the courtroom, he was his own worst enemy. Asked by his counsel, Mr Michael Morland QC, why he had not gone to the police straightaway, he said, 'I would not give them assistance for anything. I would not do it if my old man was dead.'

The explanation for his attitude is that over the years he had been in trouble with the police for a series of minor matters. Now he claimed that he had been afraid that they would accuse him of murder. He was not going to volunteer information about what he had seen. 'If there is any trouble in the village and I am nearby, the dirty end of the stick goes in my hand.'

Later, cross-examined by Mr Colin Nicholls QC for the Crown, Luckhurst admitted that he felt some anger towards Miss Marshall's killer. But even here, he foolishly weakened his chances.

Mr Nicholls: Do you hope that he might be caught?

Luckhurst: I could not give two hoots.

Perhaps it was immaturity: perhaps this was an illustration of what Lady Spens, who knew Luckhurst well, was talking about when she said that he was given to showing off, being 'the big "I am"'. But such a response was not calculated to impress a jury.

It has to be asked if Luckhurst, by now 18 years of age, and of good general intelligence, fully appreciated the seriousness of his position.

Luckhurst claimed that the bloodstains on the knife blade – the police found only fish scales on the handle – were there because he had used it in the shed when he found Miss Marshall. He had prodded her back with the knife; he lifted the collar of her coat with it. The reason, he explained, was that he did not wish to cover his hands with blood.

As for his clothes and shoes, there were insufficient blood traces to say precisely where the blood had come from. In any case Miss Marshall's blood group was common to 50 per cent of the population.

'It comes down to this,' Mr Justice Stocker observed on learning of the absence of finger prints and the paucity of blood evidence, 'there were no marks attributable to this defendant on anything.'

After five days the jury withdrew for two hours, returning with an unanimous guilty verdict. The judge, despite his earlier observation, referred to the 'overwhelming evidence against Luckhurst'.

'All I feel capable of saying about you,' he said, 'is that it has been noticeable that you have been totally lacking in any compassion or pity nor have you shown any signs of remorse for what happened. The sentence is one which is fixed by law. It is that you be detained during Her Majesty's pleasure.'

Thus, there was to be no limit to Peter Luckhurst's period of detention. His release would depend upon the Home Secretary. Luckhurst never admitted guilt for the murder of Gwendoline Marshall. At the time of writing he is still in prison though preparing for release.

At first sight the case against Peter Luckhurst seems cast-iron. After all, he did confess to murder; he described vividly what must have happened at Enfield Lodge; he had blood on his clothing, his shoes, his knife. But could this village nuisance's account really be believed?

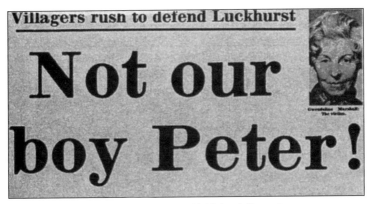

The headline in the *Kentish Express* which highlighted villagers' concerns.

Certainly, even today, there are people in Pluckley who believe him to be totally innocent. Many who knew him well, who knew his faults and who liked him in spite of those faults, cannot bring themselves to think him guilty of such an atrocious crime.

The Peter Luckhurst Defence Committee, formed immediately after the trial, sought to clear his name. To help them they enlisted the services of Brian Ford, a private detective from Hastings, who worked tirelessly on the case.

According to the Committee two defence witnesses had not been called at the time. One apparently would have testified to a man running away from Enfield Lodge at the time of the murder. The second witness would have given evidence of someone seen burning clothes on a bonfire shortly after the murder.

Certainly Peter Luckhurst was not the running man. Nor did he burn his clothes. He wore the same outfit throughout 8th October – when he was in the pub in the later morning; when he met Nikki Mannouch in the afternoon; when he sat with the Watts family that night watching TV. No one mentioned seeing blood on his clothes, yet the clothing of whoever had butchered Gwendoline Marshall must have been saturated with blood.

Similarly, had Nikki Mannouch been responsible for the murder he too would have been bloodied when he met Luckhurst that afternoon. Yet in all these years he has never been accused by the convicted man.

As for the knife in the drawer, Luckhurst's supporters wondered how it had been conveyed home. Held out in the hand, for all the world to see, as Luckhurst cycled back to his house? Or in his pocket? But his pocket was not bloodstained.

Furthermore, Peter Luckhurst was not a money grubber. If he wanted money he would call on Lady Spens or the local farmers or Miss Marshall and offer to work. According to his supporters, murder for money was just not in Peter Luckhurst's character.

And finally, what of the two significant omissions in the confession? Why had Luckhurst not mentioned cutting Miss Marshall's throat when he had given so much other significant detail? Was it because he had not seen that her throat had been slit? And why had he not said that as he roamed the house, dragging the old woman with him, he had taken her into the downstairs lavatory where bloodstains were discovered? Was it because, as he said later, he did not know of the existence of the lavatory?

According to the Defence Committee, Peter Luckhurst omitted to mention these matters because he had not committed the murder.

Over several years the Defence Committee tried to re-open the case. Brian Ford worked on the evidence. The local MP's services were called upon. In 1981 there was a reconstruction of the case on TV. In 1984 the *Sunday Times* published an in-depth account of the murder, concluding that Luckhurst was not the murderer but that he might have been present as an accomplice or a bystander.

In June 1991 Granada TV homed in with *In Suspicious Circumstances*, a programme which once more presented the uncertainties of the evidence and which led the Home Office to call for another report on the case. After nearly two years, in which hopes were raised, the report was sent to the Home Office but the decision was reached to take no further action.

So then, the truth of the matter? That is elusive. The case is riddled with questions. But local people still support Peter Luckhurst and some will even say that they have a good idea who slew Gwendoline Marshall so barbarously in her garden shed.

Others have suggested that Luckhurst was present for at least part of the time. They say that he and another person had gone to Enfield Lodge intending to commit a robbery, and that when matters got out of hand Luckhurst ran away in a panic, leaving Gwendoline Marshall to die at another's hand. But is it credible that Peter Luckhurst has suffered long imprisonment and all the while protected the guilty man?

Despite all the investigations, the cruel and savage murder at Pluckley remains a mystery.

14

THE
LETTER BOMB

The murder of Barbara Harrold at Ightham,
May 1984

During the morning of Monday 21st May 1984 the postman delivered a brown paper parcel to Old Cottage in The Street, Ightham. On a white label were written the words, 'Fragile – with care'. It was tied with a red ribbon and addressed to Mrs Barbara Harrold. As she was not at home the housekeeper, Mrs Rootes, left it on the sitting room table.

When Barbara Harrold returned from shopping at about midday, she took the parcel through to the kitchen at the back of the house. It must have been a surprise, a pleasant surprise perhaps, to receive a parcel tied with red ribbon. Perhaps it was from the grandchildren.

A fierce explosion rocked the house, blew out the windows and ripped the tiles off the work surfaces and walls. The detonator, in a manic upward trajectory, embedded itself in the ceiling.

And Barbara Harrold, a 53 year old housewife, lay on her kitchen floor, her hand torn off, her stomach and head severely injured. She was to die the following Sunday in hospital at Canterbury. The cause of death was given as heart failure.

Was it gas? A boiler, perhaps? But such obvious causes were soon dismissed. It was something more sinister, that much was plain. Mrs Rootes, found later wandering in shock outside the house, had the presence of mind to phone the police. A bomb disposal unit was summoned, and as forensic scientists sifted through the debris of the wrecked kitchen, police made house-to-house enquiries.

Members of the anti-terrorist squad came to Old Cottage. Experts were soon of the opinion that whoever had made the bomb had a

The results of the explosion at the Harrolds' house. (Alex Watson – *Sevenoaks Chronicle*)

distinct expertise. The bomber had packed a nine inch metal cylinder with high explosive, a detonator and nails. At the inquest on 12th July, Detective Superintendent David Surridge was to tell the court: 'I couldn't say whether it was meant to kill but its size and make-up indicate that it was designed to cause maximum harm.' He was

116

Roseacre sub-post office, where the bomb was posted to Mrs Harrold.

describing a fearsome weapon, an instrument of the cruellest design, the type of pipe-bomb favoured by terrorist groups. If it did not kill, it would maim horribly.

But what possible explanation could there be for such an outrage? Was it something to do with Gordon Harrold's business? He had a factory on the Platt Industrial Estate at nearby Borough Green where he manufactured polystyrene packaging for arms. Was it something to do with his MOD contracts? Had terrorists chosen to target him?

A piece of brown paper found amidst the wreckage yielded a significant lead. On it was a stamp. And a postmark. The police now knew that the parcel had been handed in at Roseacre sub-post office at Bearsted on Friday 18th May.

On 28th May a photofit was issued of a smartly dressed man, aged between 55 and 65 and about 5′ 8″ tall. He was described as stocky and of healthy appearance; he had brown hair and was wearing a sports jacket. The suspect's name was not given.

In the first week in June, Kent Police searched a house in Maidstone. The press was to claim that bomb-making equipment was found there although this was later denied by the police. Nevertheless, their quarry had stayed in that house with relatives. Still not naming him, the police announced that 'he is known to be an Englishman who was in possession of a Spanish registered car'.

The *Times* headline of 6th June reads: 'Bomb inquiry moves to Spain'. Two days later, the *Sevenoaks Chronicle* optimistically stated its view that 'the net is closing on the man police believe to have murdered Mrs Barbara Harrold'. Interpol and the Spanish police were cooperating with their British counterparts.

More information concerning the mystery man trickled out. It was now said that he had bought the Harrolds' former holiday home at Denia in Spain. It transpired that there had been some acrimonious correspondence several months after the house purchase. The Harrolds had received what the press described as 'hate mail', apparently over some outstanding local tax in Spain for which they believed they had no responsibility. Had some personal annoyance over a relatively minor matter grown into a murderous obsession?

In November 1984, at the request of Kent Police, 50 year old Keith Raymond Cottingham was arrested at Denia at the former holiday home of the Harrolds. He was charged with the illegal possession of firearms. It was hoped that this would lead to his extradition but after some time in custody he was released. A Home Office spokesman said at the time that although a new extradition treaty was being negotiated by the two governments, he held out little hope of Cottingham's return to the United Kingdom.

Cottingham has been described as an extremely practical man. He is said to be very clever with his hands, able to work metal, operate a lathe. At times, farmers in the Folkestone area where he used to live would call on his services. If, for example, they had an especially recalcitrant tree trunk they wished to be rid of, they would send for Cottingham to remove it. He had a particular skill with explosives.

As matters stand, no one has yet been brought before any court charged with this murder. A family, in the most unlikely of places, has suffered a numbing tragedy. Barbara Harrold, that most unlikely victim, was no chance casualty. That is what makes this crime so appalling, worse perhaps than many of those which take more life. The murderer knew the potential of his bomb; he knew the identity of his victim.

To date, the police's sole suspect remains in Spain. No Home Secretary has been able to prise him from there. Meanwhile, Kent Police hope that some day they may have the opportunity to question him.

15

DEATH OF A VERY
SPECIAL MAN

The death of John Fordham at West Kingsdown,
January 1985

Early evening. Dark already this raw winter day. Two men, hooded, enter the grounds, burrowing under the security fence, avoiding the electronic surveillance. They make their way stealthily through the trees, then pause to take their bearings. Ahead of them is the house, a hundred yards or so up the floodlit drive. This house belies its mock-modest name, Hollywood Cottage. It is no cottage: it is a handsome modern ten-bedroomed mansion, fitting for its 20 acres, fitting for its millionaire owner.

The intruders crouch on the damp earth, waiting. Soon, after the months of planning, it will be over. They will have the gold. They know it is in the house. Not long now.

But too long – here come the dogs. Three of them. Rottweilers. Snuffling the men out, barking as they come, advancing, retreating, curling their lips, baring their teeth. Menacing. And threatening to ruin the plan, blow it all apart.

Now someone has come out of the house. He calls the dogs, shines a torch, speaks to others.

If these dogs don't stop... One of the men withdraws cautiously. Perhaps they will follow him and quieten down, then leave. But they don't. These are guard dogs. They are not put off their work as simply as that.

And now the two men are separated. And the one who has retreated is out of contact with the other.

Shortly after, there is a struggle in the bushes, under the trees in the damp of early evening. One man is fatally injured. On the cold January earth, he gasps out his life, ten stab wounds in his body, two in the heart.

*　　*　　*

Fourteen months earlier, in November 1983, armed men had over-powered the guards and forced their way into the Brinks-Mat warehouse at Heathrow Airport. Dousing the keyholders with petrol, they threatened to set them alight if the keys to the vault were not handed over.

The gang escaped with 6,800 gold ingots valued at £26 million. It was Britain's biggest robbery, masterfully executed. Lloyd's, called on to make the largest settlement for a robbery in British insurance history, were to offer a reward of £2 million.

In the succeeding months, the police made some headway, bringing four men to trial. One was acquitted, another given a six-year sentence; two received 25 years. Little of the gold was recovered.

Nevertheless, there was considerable police activity. The specialist surveillance branch, C11, was involved. Their activities, which are usually protected from the public gaze, concentrate on major drug dealers, terrorists and the criminal elite. They were aware of the robbers' principal difficulty regarding the Brinks-Mat bullion. There were three tons to be got rid of, each of the 6,800 ingots bearing an identification mark. C11 focused on the gold-laundering operation.

By late 1984, the intelligence seekers identified the mastermind behind the laundering as Kenneth Noye, variously described as a property dealer and builder, a man who claimed to have made his money after leaving the printing trade at the age of 23. Now in his mid-thirties, he had £3.2 million in offshore accounts.

Noye's scheme was to re-smelt the gold in order to remove the identification marks and then to dispose of it in small parcels on the legitimate gold market using bogus documentation. He was also using false documents to suggest that he had paid VAT on the gold he was selling. This was netting an additional 12% on the price of the stolen gold.

The laundering operation was conducted from West Kingsdown where in recent years Noye had built Hollywood Cottage. His principal courier, Barry Reader, a man wanted by the police for burglary, carried gold from Noye to Islington where Thomas Adams and two others conveyed it to the West Country. At Lansdown, in a converted Georgian coachhouse, and at Scadlynn Bullion Ltd, owned by Garth

Chappell, the gold was re-smelted; £11 million of Brinks-Mat gold had passed along this chain.

It was a vast and complex operation. No banks appear to have been unduly surprised by the considerable amounts of money suddenly going into accounts and then just as promptly being withdrawn. On one occasion, so much was taken out from West Country banks that the Bank of England's aid had to be enlisted. Yet nothing of this seems to have furrowed the brows of the banking community.

C11, however, were gradually accumulating enough information about Noye's operation. By January 1985 they were ready to close it down and members of the Metropolitan Police, local forces and C11 prepared to raid addresses in London, the West Country and Kent.

On 22nd January a 'hide' was made in the bushes of a religious retreat opposite the gates of Hollywood Cottage. From here, using a CCTV camera concealed in a bird box, Noye and his associates were kept under observation.

On the evening of 26th January, after search warrants had been obtained, Detective Constables Neil Murphy and John Fordham were detailed to enter the grounds of Hollywood Cottage. They were to observe and report back by radio any activity in the grounds or house. Noye and Reader as well as their wives were known to be inside.

Both C11 men were experienced. John Fordham, 45 years old, was described as 'perhaps the most experienced and best trained surveillance officer in the country'. Naturally he was there. This was an operation of major importance.

At 6.25 pm Fordham radioed to his colleagues outside the gates that hostile dogs had approached him and Murphy. Two minutes later he reported that a man with a torch had come out of the house, calling the dogs.

Murphy, anxious not to prejudice the operation, after failing to quieten the Rottweilers with yeast tablets, retreated towards the gates, hoping to draw the dogs after him. He was unsuccessful in this and warned the officers outside.

Ten minutes later, at 6.37 pm, Murphy reported hearing a man shouting, 'Show us your ID then' and 'I'll blow your head off'.

At 6.40 pm, in response to Murphy's call, police entered the grounds in numbers. A member of the Flying Squad, Detective Constable David Manning, found Noye with a shotgun standing over Fordham.

'There were three dogs,' Manning was to say at Noye's trial, 'pulling and tugging at his [Fordham's] clothing. I shouted out, "I am a police

Police activity at Hollywood Cottage, after the death of Detective Constable John Fordham.
(Alex Watson – *Sevenoaks Chronicle*)

officer". I held out my warrant card. The defendant took several steps towards me and said, "F - - - off or I'll do you as well." '

Ignoring Noye and his dogs, Manning knelt down to tend to the fatally wounded policeman.

'He's done me. He stabbed me,' Fordham told him.

Noye ran off towards the house but was followed by police who placed him under arrest. Reader, presumably warned by Noye, escaped from the house but was later picked up on the main road trying to hitch a lift.

A search of Hollywood Cottage uncovered eleven bars of gold, valued at £100,000, concealed in a gully in the patio. £69,000 in cash was also found. Built into the swimming pool were secret compartments, empty at the time.

Noye denied at once that the gold came from the Brinks-Mat robbery. He claimed that it was smuggled gold from Kuwait and Brazil destined for the Netherlands. But the questioning that night had more to do with the death of John Fordham.

At Bromley police station, Noye asked to speak privately to Detective Chief Superintendent Brian Boyce, the officer in charge of the surveillance operation. Before speaking, Noye demanded that no notes be taken. He insisted also on searching Boyce's briefcase in case a tape-recorder was hidden in there.

'Noye told me he was a very rich man,' Boyce reported later. 'He wanted to give some money to the policeman's wife and family.' Boyce was then offered £1 million, payable to any bank in the world, 'if I made sure he did not go to prison.'

Boyce replied that all he wanted was to know the whereabouts of the rest of the Brinks-Mat bullion. 'If I told you that, I am a dead man,' Noye told him.

Meanwhile, the raids, 'real Sweeney stuff' according to the press, had netted a couple of dozen suspects throughout the country.

Charged with murder, Noye was tried at the Central Criminal Court in November 1985. Noye's account of the killing was that he had heard the dogs barking and had gone out to investigate. He had taken a torch and a knife which he had been using earlier to clean his car battery.

He told the court that when he reached the dogs, a masked man suddenly loomed up in front of him. 'I could just see two eye holes,' he said. 'I just froze in horror. I thought it was my lot. I was going to be a dead man. I just thought that was it.'

'The man did not say a word. Immediately he caught me across the face with what I thought was a weapon. I immediately put my hand up to my face, grabbed his hand and started stabbing with the knife as fast as I could. I struck at his front all of five times. As far as I was concerned I was fighting for my life. He was overwhelmingly on top of me. He looked grotesque, big. I fell down. The masked man came on top of me and I struck at him again.'

Before entering Fordham's body up to the hilt, Noye's knife cut through five layers of clothing: a camouflage suit, a waterproof suit, a jumper, sweatshirt and vest. To penetrate these layers required blows delivered with the force of a punch.

By then, Reader and Noye's wife, Brenda, had come down the path. Noye went over to them and took a shotgun from Reader. 'I did not want him to get away in case he came back another time when I was not there to sort Brenda and the children out.' In Noye's dark world, there were always awful possibilities.

Now, standing over the policeman, Noye demanded to see his ID, threatening to blow his head off. Fordham, mortally injured but still anxious not to betray the imminent police raid, answered that he was in the SAS, on manoeuvres. He took off the mask.

Noye now asked his wife to call an ambulance and to bring him a camera. He intended to photograph the stricken man. 'Because he said he was SAS, I wanted to make sure my account was put right when the public enquiry came,' he explained. 'I would show the mask beside him.' Cool thinking at such a time.

Later, in the house, Detective Sergeant Yeoman asked Noye what had happened.

'Old Bill or no, he had no f - - - - - - business being here,' he is reported as saying.

'Do you realise that police officer you stabbed is dying?' Yeoman asked him.

'He should not have been on my property,' is Noye's alleged response. 'I hope he f - - - - - - dies.'

'I could not believe how cheaply he treated life,' Yeoman told the court.

'Yeah,' Noye had said. 'I did him before he took the knife from me. I did not know he was a police officer.'

And this was the centre of Noye's defence, his unawareness that the man who loomed up at him was a policeman. 'You know how he was dressed,' he said to Detective Inspector Robert Brightwell, shortly after his arrest. 'What would you have done? I have a wife and family. You go and see someone like him. It is you or him. If he had had a badge, it would not have happened.'

Kenneth Noye was a major criminal and by his deeds and life-style he did not merit any respect from the majority of people. John Fordham was not a millionaire. He was a highly respected policeman, a genuinely worthy man. The heart will always opt for Fordham. The head, too, for it is the Fordhams that this world needs. Yet the case presented no easy solution for the jury.

John Mathew QC, counsel for Noye, told the jury: 'Any person is entitled to defend himself which means in the context of this case that if you reasonably think that someone is going to attack you, and even more so if someone does attack you, you are entitled to defend yourself.'

The jury had to decide whether a man who had set the law at naught was innocent of the murder of an infinitely more decent man. Noye had even been accused of kicking the dying Fordham but that was not the case against him, not the issue.

Mr Justice Caulfield, summing up, also reminded the jury of a man's right to defend himself 'and you are entitled to use such force as is reasonable in the circumstances to prevent the attack'. Notice the words 'reasonable in the circumstances'.

The judge went on to recall to the jury their visit to Hollywood Cottage at the beginning of the trial. 'Were those grounds desecrated by the vicious murder of a man on 26th January? Or was there a man killed lawfully because he was an aggressor who had petrified the owner, and the owner, almost paralysed with fear, killed him and in his terror stabbed him not once, twice or thrice, but ten times?'

The jury acquitted Noye. In their view he acted as a householder, frightened by an apparently dangerous trespasser. He had simply defended himself.

Leaving court, Noye called out to the jury, 'May God bless you for ever because that is what I am, not guilty.'

This is in marked contrast to his alleged comment to the jury at the conclusion of his later trial in connection with the stolen gold. After an eleven-week trial the jury found him guilty; this time he called out, 'I hope you all die of cancer.'

In addition to a 14-year prison sentence, Noye was fined £500,000 and his £3.2 million offshore accounts were frozen. Civil proceedings were taken against him by Customs and Excise for the VAT fraud and by Brinks-Mat for their losses. He was refused legal aid.

In 1987 Noye received a further four years to run concurrently with the other sentence. This time he had been found guilty of the possession of antique Meissen porcelain stolen from the Kent home of the Earl of Darnley. In all, Noye served eight years in prison.

Brian Reader was charged with receiving £66,000, knowing it was stolen. He was sentenced to two years and fined £3,000. Other gang members were given various terms of imprisonment although not all were brought to justice. Nor was all of the Brinks-Mat gold retrieved.

There was no public enquiry into the tragic outcome of the West Kingsdown raid. In the view of the police authorities and of the then Home Secretary, Douglas Hurd, the operation had been professionally and properly carried out.

In September 1987, a memorial to John Fordham was erected on West Kingsdown Green. On this occasion Sir Peter Imbert, Commissioner of the Metropolitan Police, said it was right that people should mourn and feel angry at John Fordham's death. He was, said the Commissioner, 'a very special man, one who rightly cherished ordinary hopes and ambitions, gave all he could in the search for a society free from crime.'

Since then, the name of John Fordham has probably slipped from the public's mind. Kenneth Noye's has not.

After leaving prison Noye resumed his lavish lifestyle; so much for the intentions to strip him of his assets. His name very quickly cropped up once more in a number of major police investigations. One was into a scheme to steal £800 million from cash machines. Another, in 1996, led to a policeman named John Donald being jailed for eleven years for offering to sell information to criminals. Noye, however, was not charged in connection with these or other offences.

The police would now like to question Noye about the murder in May 1996 of a young man on a motorway slip road not far from West Kingsdown. Here, 21 year old Stephen Cameron was stabbed to death during a roadside altercation, the press dubbing the case 'The M25 Road Rage Murder'. After some weeks of investigation police stated that they wished to interview Noye about the matter. But he had disappeared.

From time to time there have been reported sightings of Noye: it is said he has been seen in northern Cyprus, in Marbella and in St Petersburg. There are claims that he has stayed in a timeshare in Lanzarote where his good friend John 'Goldfinger' Palmer owns a considerable amount of property.

So what sort of man is he, this high-living criminal, this absent millionaire? In answer to that question put by a journalist, a policeman replied: 'To a middle class boy like you? Absolutely your worst bloody nightmare.'

Justly or not, there are several families who would support that judgement.

INDEX